little knitted
CREATURES

LEISURE ARTS, INC.
Little Rock, Arkansas

EDITORIAL STAFF
Editor-in-Chief: Susan White Sullivan
Knit and Crochet Publications Director: Debra Nettles
Special Projects Director: Susan Frantz Wiles
Senior Prepress Director: Mark Hawkins
Art Publications Director: Rhonda Shelby
Technical Editor: Linda Daley
Contributing Editors: Sarah J. Green and Joan Beebe
Editorial Writer: Susan McManus Johnson
Art Category Manager: Lora Puls
Graphic Artist: Becca Snider
Production Artist: Janie Wright
Imaging Technicians: Stephanie Johnson
  and Mark R. Potter
Photography Director: Katherine Laughlin
Contributing Photographer: Ken West
Contributing Photostylist: Sondra Daniel
Publishing Systems Administrator: Becky Riddle
Publishing Systems Assistants: Clint Hanson
  and Keiji Yumoto
Mac IT Specialist: Robert Young

BUSINESS STAFF
Vice President and Chief Operations Officer:
  Tom Siebenmorgen
Director of Finance and Administration:
  Laticia Mull Dittrich
Vice President, Sales and Marketing: Pam Stebbins
Sales Director: Martha Adams
Marketing Director: Margaret Reinold
Creative Services Director: Jeff Curtis
Information Technology Director: Hermine Linz
Controller: Francis Caple
Vice President, Operations: Jim Dittrich
Comptroller, Operations: Rob Thieme
Retail Customer Service Manager: Stan Raynor
Print Production Manager: Fred F. Pruss

Library of Congress Control Number: 2010925825
ISBN-13: 978-1-60900-014-1

10 9 8 7 6 5 4 3 2 1

table of
CONTENTS

MEET THE CUTEST CREATURES IN THE ANIMAL KINGDOM!

They're cuddly, fun to knit, and some of them are surprisingly human (just don't tell them that!).

These little knitted folk are truly amazing. Some of them have jobs. They have friends. And they certainly have adventures! That's because they're amigurumi, knitted dolls inspired by the Japanese craft trend. Amy Gaines is the creative force behind AmyGaines.com, the online pattern company that introduced knitters and crocheters around the world to Amy's friendly yarn-based life forms.

If you like to crochet, you'll also want to meet Amy's fun crocheted critters! Visit leisurearts.com to buy leaflets #4271 Cute Little Animals and #5125 More Cute Little Animals. With amigurumi, the fun never ends!

friendly
SEA-CIETY

Surf's up! Which means the Friendly Sea-ciety is coming ashore for some fun! Cletus Claw, Tentacle Terry, Big Blue, and Shelly Green are four good buddies who always have a whale of a time no matter where they are—but they especially love to hit the beach when the tide is rolling in. That's because they like to watch the surfer dudes wipe out. The only thing the Sea-ciety likes better is when they go back in the water later the same day. By then, the surfers are weary from hours of shooting the curls. Chances are good they've been trading the latest scary shark tales while they paddle in the water, waiting for the next big roller. With just a wee nudge to their feet from the Sea-ciety folk, the dudes are back up on their boards in an instant. It's a good thing the surfers don't know what a giggling sea turtle sounds like. The indignity could dampen their spirits.

There are crabby people in the world, to be sure, but the crabbiest folks may be the ones who are born to the title. Cletus Claw is a snappy little fellow who's quick to pinch first and ask questions later. At least he used to be. Now that Shelly Green's a regular part of the gang, Cletus has been on his best behavior for quite a while. He gets all googly-eyed and quiet when she's around. It's not that he's shy, it's just that he's afraid he'll be his own naturally cranky self and say something that will offend her. The guys kid him about it, but Cletus is most definitely smitten.

cletus
CLAW

Finished Size: 3¹/₈" (8 cm) tall

MATERIALS

Medium Weight Yarn
[3¹/₂ ounces, 170 yards
(100 grams, 156 meters) per skein]:
   Dk Red - 1 skein
Straight knitting needles, size 4 (3.5 mm)
Stitch holder **or** safety pin
Yarn needle
Polyester stuffing
9 mm Black doll eyes - 2

Techniques used:
• Invisible increase
   (*Fig. 1, page 110*)
• K2 tog (*Fig. 3, page 110*)
• P2 tog (*Fig. 5, page 110*)

BODY
With Dk Red and leaving a long end for sewing, cast on 48 sts.

Row 1 (Wrong side): Purl across.

Row 2: Knit across.

Rows 3-17: Repeat Rows 1 and 2, 7 times; then repeat Row 1 once **more**.

Row 18: (K2 tog, K4) across: 40 sts.

Row 19: Purl across.

Row 20: (K2 tog, K3) across: 32 sts.

Row 21: Purl across.

Row 22: (K2 tog, K2) across: 24 sts.

Row 23: Purl across.

Row 24: (K2 tog, K1) across: 16 sts.

Row 25: P2 tog across: 8 sts.

Cut Dk Red leaving a 12" (30.5 cm) length for sewing.

Thread yarn needle with end and weave through remaining sts; pull tightly and sew end of rows together halfway.

Using photo as a guide for placement, page 6, attach eyes. Finish sewing seam, stuffing Body as you go.

BELLY
With Dk Red, cast on 8 sts.

Row 1 (Wrong side)**:** Purl across.

Row 2 (Increase row): Work invisible increase, knit across to last st, work invisible increase, K1: 10 sts.

Instructions continued on page 8.

Rows 3-8: Repeat Rows 1 and 2, 3 times: 16 sts.

Row 9: Purl across.

Row 10: Knit across.

Rows 11-14: Repeat Rows 9 and 10 twice.

Row 15: Purl across.

Row 16 (Decrease row)**:** K2 tog, knit across to last 2 sts, K2 tog: 14 sts.

Rows 17-22: Repeat Rows 15 and 16, 3 times: 8 sts.

Bind off remaining sts in **purl**, leaving a 15" (38 cm) length for sewing.

Thread yarn needle with end and sew Belly to Body opening, adding additional stuffing if needed.

CLAW (Make 2)
FIRST SIDE
With Dk Red, leaving a long end for sewing and beginning at Body edge, cast on 6 sts.

Row 1 (Wrong side)**:** Purl across.

Row 2: Knit across.

Row 3: Purl across.

Row 4 (Increase row)**:** Knit across to last st, work invisible increase, K1: 7 sts.

Row 5: Purl across.

Rows 6-11: Repeat Rows 4 and 5, 3 times: 10 sts.

Small Pincher
Row 1: Work invisible increase, K2, K2 tog, slip last 6 sts onto st holder or safety pin: 4 sts.

Row 2: Purl across.

Row 3: K2 tog twice: 2 sts.

Row 4: P2 tog: one st.

Cut Dk Red and pull end through remaining st to finish off.

Large Pincher
Slip 6 sts from st holder or safety pin onto empty needle.

Row 1 (Right side)**:** With Dk Red, knit across to last st, work invisible increase, K1: 7 sts.

Row 2: Purl across.

Row 3: Knit across to last st, work invisible increase, K1: 8 sts.

Row 4: Purl across.

Row 5: Knit across.

Row 6: Purl across.

Row 7: K6, K2 tog: 7 sts.

Row 8: P2 tog, P5: 6 sts.

Row 9: K4, K2 tog: 5 sts.

Row 10: P2 tog, P3: 4 sts.

Row 11: K2, K2 tog: 3 sts.

Row 12: P2 tog, P1: 2 sts.

Row 13: K2 tog: one st.

Cut Dk Red and pull end through remaining st to finish off.

SECOND SIDE
With Dk Red, leaving a long end for sewing and beginning at Body edge, cast on 6 sts.

Row 1 (Wrong side)**:** Purl across.

Row 2: Knit across.

Row 3: Purl across.

Row 4 (Increase row): Work invisible increase, knit across: 7 sts.

Row 5: Purl across.

Rows 6-11: Repeat Rows 4 and 5, 3 times: 10 sts.

Large Pincher
Row 1: Work invisible increase, K6, slip last 4 sts onto st holder or safety pin: 7 sts.

Row 2: Purl across.

Row 3: Work invisible increase, knit across: 8 sts.

Row 4: Purl across.

Row 5: Knit across.

Row 6: Purl across.

Row 7: K2 tog, K6: 7 sts.

Row 8: P5, P2 tog: 6 sts.

Row 9: K2 tog, K4: 5 sts.

Row 10: P3, P2 tog: 4 sts.

Row 11: K2 tog, K2: 3 sts.

Row 12: P1, P2 tog: 2 sts.

Row 13: K2 tog: one st.

Cut Dk Red and pull end through remaining st to finish off.

Small Pincher
Slip 4 sts from st holder or safety pin onto empty needle.

Row 1 (Right side): With Dk Red, K2 tog, K1, work invisible increase, K1.

Row 2: Purl across.

Row 3: K2 tog twice: 2 sts.

Row 4: P2 tog: one st.

Cut Dk Red and pull end through remaining st to finish off.

Place First Side and Second Side with **wrong** sides together. Sew pieces together, stuffing Claw lightly before closing.

Using photo as a guide for placement, sew Claws to Body, having Small Pincher toward front of Crab.

LEG (Make 8)
With Dk Red, leaving a long end for sewing and beginning at Body edge, cast on 6 sts.

Row 1 (Wrong side): Purl across.

Row 2: Knit across.

Row 3: Purl across.

Rows 4 and 5: Repeat Rows 2 and 3.

Row 6: Work invisible increase, K1, K2 tog twice, work invisible increase, K1.

Row 7: Purl across.

Rows 8-11: Repeat Rows 6 and 7 twice.

Row 12: K2 tog across: 3 sts.

Cut Dk Red leaving a 12" (30.5 cm) length for sewing.

Thread yarn needle with end and weave through remaining sts; pull tightly and sew end of rows together, stuffing Leg lightly. Sew 4 Legs to each side of Crab, using photo as a guide for placement.

Talk about your complex personalities! At any given time, Terry has at least four different projects on his hands—uh, tentacles. He can multi-task like no one else on earth—or, um, at sea. Terry likes to eat oysters, tease moray eels, and open lobster traps. As a member of the Friendly Sea-ciety, he enjoys the occasional practical joke. His best prank is simple, just waiting behind a clump of coral for a small school of fish to swim by. He taps them all at once on their fins, and then stifles his laughter when they swoosh around and look at each other, trying to figure out who did it.

tentacle
TERRY

Finished Size: 3¹/₂" (9 cm) tall

MATERIALS

Medium Weight Yarn
[3¹/₂ ounces, 170 yards
(100 grams, 156 meters) per skein]:
  Purple - 1 skein
Straight knitting needles, size 4 (3.5 mm)
Stitch holder **or** safety pin
Yarn needle
Polyester stuffing
9 mm Black doll eyes - 2

Techniques used:
• Invisible increase *(Fig. 1, page 110)*
• K2 tog *(Fig. 3, page 110)*
• P2 tog *(Fig. 5, page 110)*

BODY
With Purple and leaving a long end for sewing, cast on 24 sts.

Row 1 (Wrong side)**:** Purl across.

Row 2: Knit across.

Rows 3-5: Repeat Rows 1 and 2 once, then repeat Row 1 once **more.**

Row 6: (Work invisible increase, K2) across: 36 sts.

Row 7: Purl across.

Row 8: Knit across.

Rows 9-25: Repeat Rows 7 and 8, 8 times; then repeat Row 7 once **more.**

Row 26: (K2 tog, K2) across: 27 sts.

Row 27: Purl across.

Row 28: (K2 tog, K1) across: 18 sts.

Row 29: Purl across.

Row 30: K2 tog across: 9 sts.

Cut Purple leaving a 12" (30.5 cm) length for sewing.

Instructions continued on page 12.

Thread yarn needle with end and weave through remaining sts; pull tightly and sew end of rows together halfway.

Using photo as a guide for placement, page 10, attach eyes. Finish sewing seam, stuffing Body as you go.

BELLY
With Purple, cast on 6 sts.

Row 1 (Wrong side)**:** Purl across.

Row 2: Work invisible increase, K5, work invisible increase, K1: 8 sts.

Row 3: Purl across.

Row 4: Knit across.

Rows 5-7: Repeat Rows 3 and 4 once, then repeat Row 3 once **more**.

Row 8: K2 tog, K4, K2 tog: 6 sts.

Bind off remaining sts in **purl**, leaving a 15" (38 cm) length for sewing.

Thread yarn needle with end and sew Belly to Body opening, adding additional stuffing if needed.

LEGS
DOUBLE CURL (Make 4)
With Purple and beginning at Body edge, cast on 30 sts.

Row 1 (Wrong side)**:** Purl across.

Row 2: K 10, (work invisible increase, K1) across: 50 sts.

Row 3: Purl across.

Rows 4 and 5: Knit across.

Row 6: Purl across.

Row 7: K2 tog 20 times, K 10: 30 sts.

Bind off remaining sts in **purl**, leaving a long end for sewing.

SINGLE CURL (Make 4)
With Purple and beginning at Body edge, cast on 30 sts.

Row 1 (Wrong side)**:** Purl across.

Row 2: K 20, (work invisible increase, K1) across: 40 sts.

Row 3: Purl across.

Rows 4 and 5: Knit across.

Row 6: Purl across.

Row 7: K2 tog 10 times, K 20: 30 sts.

Bind off remaining sts in **purl**, leaving a long end for sewing.

Thread yarn needle with long end. Fold Legs lengthwise and sew cast on edge and bind off edge together.

Using photo as a guide for placement, sew Legs to Body, alternating Single Curl and Double Curl Legs.

When Shelly was just a hatchling in the Galapagos, her life was truly chaotic. There were hungry lizards on the beach where she hatched and a lot of hungry sea mammals in the water. Shelly somehow got past those hazards and now makes herself at home on the beaches of California. Sure, she has to watch for boats and the occasional fisherman, but mostly life is calmer now. Recently, she posed for photos with a celebrity spokesman for environmental issues. Everyone keeps telling her she's a real bathing beauty.

shelly
GREEN

Instructions begin on page 14.

Finished Size: 2¹/₂" (6.5 cm) tall

MATERIALS

Medium Weight Yarn
[3¹/₂ ounces, 170 yards
(100 grams, 156 meters) per skein]:
  Green - 1 skein
  Lt Green - 1 skein
Straight knitting needles, size 4 (3.5 mm)
Yarn needle
Polyester stuffing
6 mm Black doll eyes - 2

Techniques used:
• Invisible increase *(Fig. 1, page 110)*
• K2 tog *(Fig. 3, page 110)*
• P2 tog *(Fig. 5, page 110)*

SHELL

With Green and leaving a long end for sewing, cast on 48 sts.

Row 1 (Wrong side)**:** Purl across.

Row 2: Knit across.

Rows 3-11: Repeat Rows 1 and 2, 4 times; then repeat Row 1 once **more**.

Row 12: (K2 tog, K2) across: 36 sts.

Row 13: Purl across.

Row 14: (K2 tog, K1) across: 24 sts.

Row 15: Purl across.

Row 16: K2 tog across: 12 sts.

Row 17: P2 tog across: 6 sts.

Cut Green leaving a 12" (30.5 cm) length for sewing.

Thread yarn needle with end and weave through remaining sts; pull tightly and sew end of rows together.

BELLY

With Lt Green, cast on 8 sts.

Row 1 (Wrong side)**:** Purl across.

Row 2 (Increase row)**:** Work invisible increase, knit across to last st, work invisible increase, K1: 10 sts.

Rows 3-8: Repeat Rows 1 and 2, 3 times: 16 sts.

Row 9: Purl across.

Row 10: Knit across.

Rows 11-14: Repeat Rows 9 and 10 twice.

Row 15: Purl across.

Row 16 (Decrease row)**:** K2 tog, knit across to last 2 sts, K2 tog: 14 sts.

Rows 17-22: Repeat Rows 15 and 16, 3 times: 8 sts.

Bind off remaining sts in **purl**, leaving a 15" (38 cm) length for sewing.

Thread yarn needle with end and sew Belly to Shell opening, stuffing as you go.

HEAD

With Lt Green, leaving a long end for sewing and beginning at neck, cast on 16 sts.

Row 1 (Wrong side)**:** Purl across.

Row 2: Knit across.

Row 3: Purl across.

Row 4: Work invisible increase, K2, work invisible increase, K3, work invisible increase, K2, work invisible increase, K9: 20 sts.

Row 5: Purl across.

Row 6: Work invisible increase, K4, work invisible increase, K3, work invisible increase, K4, work invisible increase, K9: 24 sts.

Row 7: Purl across.

Row 8: Knit across.

Row 9: Purl across.

Row 10: K2 tog across: 12 sts.

Row 11: P2 tog across: 6 sts.

Cut Lt Green leaving a 12" (30.5 cm) length for sewing.

Thread yarn needle with end and weave through remaining sts; pull tightly and sew end of rows together halfway.

Using photo as a guide for placement, page 13, attach eyes. Finish sewing seam, stuffing Head as you go. Sew Head to Shell and Belly.

FLIPPER (Make 2)
With Lt Green and beginning at Belly edge, cast on 12 sts.

Row 1 (Wrong side)**:** Purl across.

Row 2: Knit across.

Row 3: Purl across.

Row 4: Work invisible increase, K4, K2 tog twice, K3, work invisible increase, K1.

Row 5: Purl across.

Rows 6-9: Repeat Rows 4 and 5 twice.

Row 10: K2 tog, K2, K2 tog twice, K2, K2 tog: 8 sts.

Row 11: Purl across.

Row 12: K2 tog across: 4 sts.

Cut Lt Green leaving a 12" (30.5 cm) length for sewing.

Thread yarn needle with end and weave through remaining sts; pull tightly and sew end of rows together, stuffing Flipper lightly.

Using photo as a guide, sew to each side along Belly edge, approximately ¼" (6 mm) from Head.

FOOT (Make 2)
With Lt Green and beginning at Belly edge, cast on 12 sts.

Row 1 (Wrong side)**:** Purl across.

Row 2: Knit across.

Row 3: Purl across.

Row 4: K2 tog, K2, K2 tog twice, K2, K2 tog: 8 sts.

Row 5: Purl across.

Row 6: K2 tog across: 4 sts.

Cut Lt Green leaving a 12" (30.5 cm) length for sewing.

Thread yarn needle with end and weave through remaining sts; pull tightly and sew end of rows together, stuffing Foot lightly.

Using photo as a guide, sew to each side along Belly edge, approximately 1" (2.5 cm) from Flippers.

Yes, he is a whale. And despite his name, Big Blue is a bit on the small side. But then, being a small whale has its advantages. If he were regular size, he would never be able to roll up on the beach to watch the surfers with the rest of the Friendly Sea-ciety. Or if he did, he would need an awful lot of help getting back into the water. Not true of Big Blue. With a flip of his tail, he tumbles safely back into the surf with a modest splash. In another month or so, he'll be headed out to sea for a family reunion, where his size will be the subject of teasing. But it's only because his cousins are envious. They've figured out that Big Blue's stories about beach parties aren't just fish tales, and they wish they could see all that for themselves. Just imagine humans playing in the water like dolphins—ridiculous!

big
BLUE

Finished Size: 4¹/₂" (11.5 cm) tall

MATERIALS

Medium Weight Yarn
[3¹/₂ ounces, 170 yards
(100 grams, 156 meters) per skein]:
  Dk Blue - 1 skein
  Lt Blue - 1 skein
Straight knitting needles, size 4 (3.5 mm)
Yarn needle
Polyester stuffing
9 mm Black doll eyes - 2

Techniques used:
• Invisible increase (*Fig. 1, page 110*)
• K2 tog (*Fig. 3, page 110*)
• P2 tog (*Fig. 5, page 110*)

BODY
With Dk Blue and beginning at tail,
cast on 12 sts.

Row 1 (Wrong side)**:** Purl across.

Row 2: Knit across.

Row 3: Purl across.

Row 4: ★ Work invisible increase, K5,
work invisible increase, K1; repeat from ★
once **more**: 16 sts.

Rows 5-7: Repeat Rows 1-3.

Row 8: ★ Work invisible increase, K7,
work invisible increase, K1; repeat from ★
once **more**: 20 sts.

Rows 9-11: Repeat Rows 1-3.

Row 12: ★ Work invisible increase, K9,
work invisible increase, K1; repeat from ★
once **more**: 24 sts.

Row 13: Purl across.

Row 14: Work invisible increase,
★ K5, work invisible increase, K1, work
invisible increase; repeat from ★ once
more, K 11, work invisible increase, K1:
30 sts.

Row 15: Purl across.

Instructions continued on page 18.

Row 16: Work invisible increase, ★ K7, work invisible increase, K1, work invisible increase; repeat from ★ once **more**, K 13, work invisible increase, K1: 36 sts.

Row 17: Purl across.

Row 18: Work invisible increase, ★ K9, work invisible increase, K1, work invisible increase; repeat from ★ once **more**, K 15, work invisible increase, K1: 42 sts.

Row 19: Purl across.

Row 20: Work invisible increase, ★ K 11, work invisible increase, K1, work invisible increase; repeat from ★ once **more**, K 17, work invisible increase, K1: 48 sts.

Row 21: Purl across.

Row 22: Work invisible increase, K 13, work invisible increase, K1, work invisible increase, K 13, work invisible increase, K 21: 52 sts.

Row 23: Purl across.

Row 24: Work invisible increase, K 15, work invisible increase, K1, work invisible increase, K 15, work invisible increase, K 21: 56 sts.

Row 25: Purl across.

Row 26: K 17, work invisible increase, K1, work invisible increase, K 38: 58 sts.

Row 27: Purl across.

Row 28: K 18, work invisible increase, K1, work invisible increase, K 39: 60 sts.

Row 29: Purl across.

Row 30: K 19, work invisible increase, K1, work invisible increase, K 40: 62 sts.

Row 31: Purl across.

Row 32: Knit across.

Rows 33-39: Repeat Rows 31 and 32, 3 times; then repeat Row 31 once **more**.

Row 40: K 19, K2 tog twice, K 39: 60 sts.

Row 41: Purl across.

Row 42: (K2 tog, K3) across: 48 sts.

Row 43: Purl across.

Row 44: (K2 tog, K2) across: 36 sts.

Row 45: Purl across.

Row 46: (K2 tog, K1) across: 24 sts.

Row 47: Purl across.

Row 48: K2 tog across: 12 sts.

Row 49: P2 tog across: 6 sts.

Cut Dk Blue leaving a 15" (38 cm) length for sewing.

Thread yarn needle with end and weave through remaining sts (face); pull tightly and sew end of rows together halfway.

Using photo as a guide for placement, page 16, attach eyes. Finish sewing seam, stuffing Body firmly as you go and gathering cast on edge to avoid leaving a hole.

BELLY
With Lt Blue and beginning close to face, cast on 12 sts.

Row 1 (Wrong side)**:** Purl across.

Row 2: ★ Work invisible increase, K5, work invisible increase, K1; repeat from ★ once **more**: 16 sts.

Row 3: Purl across.

Row 4: ★ Work invisible increase, K7, work invisible increase, K1; repeat from ★ once **more**: 20 sts.

Row 5: Purl across.

Row 6: Knit across.

Rows 7-16: Repeat Rows 5 and 6, 5 times.

Row 17: Purl across.

Row 18 (Decrease row): K2 tog, knit across to last 2 sts, K2 tog: 18 sts.

Rows 19-24: Repeat Rows 17 and 18, 3 times: 12 sts.

Bind off remaining sts in **purl**, leaving a 15" (38 cm) length for sewing.

Thread yarn needle with end. With **wrong** side of Belly and **right** side of Body together, and having cast on edge approximately 1" (2.5 cm) from gathered stitches on face, sew Belly to bottom of Body.

FIN (Make 4)
With Dk Blue, cast on 6 sts.

Row 1 (Wrong side): Purl across.

Row 2: Knit across.

Row 3: Purl across.

Row 4 (Increase row): Work invisible increase, knit across to last st, work invisible increase, K1: 8 sts.

Row 5: Purl across.

Rows 6 and 7: Repeat Rows 4 and 5: 10 sts.

Row 8: Knit across.

Row 9: Purl across.

Row 10: K2 tog across: 5 sts.

Cut Dk Blue leaving a 12" (30.5 cm) length for sewing.

Thread yarn needle with end and weave through remaining sts; pull tightly and sew end of rows together. Using photo as a guide for placement, sew one Fin to each side of Body and 2 Fins to gathered cast on edge at tail.

spring PARTY

....

It's Billie Waddle's birthday! Hank Lambswool and the Wren Twins spent weeks planning this party as a big surprise for Billie. They even decided to pitch in and get Billie an all-expenses-paid trip to see her favorite musician in concert. Unfortunately, they put Buster Bunny Jr. in charge of something really important. You see, Buster isn't very good at paying attention. For one thing, he forgot the party was supposed to be a surprise and told Billie about it. Billie had to calm the Wren Twins or they would have pecked Buster for blabbing. She asked them to settle their differences later, thinking that cooler heads would prevail. Sure enough, once everyone was enjoying the party, they forgot about Buster's goof. Except for Buster. He just remembered his present for Billie was supposed to be concert tickets. Now he's wondering if he can slip away while no one is looking. He doesn't want to be there when Billie opens the box of croquet wickets.

Flitter and Twitter are curious about everything. Whether it's the arrival of a new neighbor, one of Buster Bunny Jr.'s escapades, or the recipe for a birthday cake, the energetic girls are sure to be checking out the details and asking lots of questions. Wrens grow up fast, and this boisterous duo will soon be leaving the family home to explore the world outside Sunny Vale. No doubt they'll find plenty that piques their curiosity!

wren
TWINS

Finished Sizes:
Birdhouse: 6" (15 cm) tall
Bird: 2" (5 cm) tall

MATERIALS
   Medium Weight Yarn
   [6 ounces, 312 yards
   (170 grams, 285 meters) per skein]:
   Lt Green - 1 skein
   Dk Brown - 1 skein
   Brown - 1 skein
   Lt Blue - 1 skein
   Lt Pink - 1 skein
Straight knitting needles, size 4 (3.5 mm)
3" (7.5 cm) Square scrap cardboard
Felt - small amount of Dk Brown and Brown
Polyester stuffing
Sewing needle and brown thread
Yarn needle

Techniques used:
• Invisible increase
   (Fig. 1, page 110)
• K2 tog *(Fig. 3, page 110)*
• P2 tog *(Fig. 5, page 110)*

BIRDHOUSE
BASE
With Dk Brown, cast on 16 sts.

Row 1 (Wrong side)**:** Purl across.

Row 2: Knit across.

Rows 3-33: Repeat Rows 1 and 2, 15 times; then repeat Row 1 once **more**.

Bind off all sts in **purl**.

Matching cast on edge to bind off edge, fold Base in half with **wrong** side together. Cut cardboard slightly smaller than folded Base. Thread yarn needle with Dk Brown and sew all 3 sides, inserting cardboard before closing.

FRONT/BACK (Make 2)
With Lt Green, cast on 16 sts.

Row 1 (Wrong side)**:** Purl across.

Row 2: Knit across.

Rows 3-9: Repeat Rows 1 and 2, 3 times; then repeat Row 1 once **more**.

Row 10 (Increase row)**:** Work invisible increase, knit across to last st, work invisible increase, K1: 18 sts.

Row 11: Purl across.

Row 12: Knit across.

Row 13: Purl across.

Instructions continued on page 24.

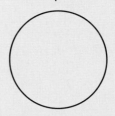

ROOF

With Dk Brown, cast on 16 sts.

Knit every row until Roof measures approximately 8" (20.5 cm) from cast on edge.

Bind off all sts in **knit**.

Thread yarn needle with Lt Green and sew Roof to house, stuffing house firmly before closing.

Trace circle pattern below and cut one piece from Dk Brown felt. Using photo as a guide for placement, sew circle to Birdhouse with needle and Brown thread.

Circle pattern

PERCH

With Dk Brown, cast on 4 sts.

Row 1 (Wrong side): Purl across.

Row 2: Knit across.

Rows 3-5: Repeat Rows 1 and 2 once, then repeat Row 1 once **more**.

Cut Dk Brown leaving a 12" (30.5 cm) length for sewing.

Rows 14-21: Repeat Rows 10-13 twice: 22 sts.

Row 22 (Decrease row): K2 tog, knit across to last 2 sts, K2 tog: 20 sts.

Row 23: Purl across.

Rows 24-39: Repeat Rows 22 and 23, 8 times: 4 sts.

Row 40: K2 tog twice: 2 sts.

Row 41: P2 tog: one st.

Cut Lt Green and pull end through remaining st to finish off.

SIDE (Make 2)

With Lt Green, cast on 14 sts.

Row 1 (Wrong side): Purl across.

Row 2: Knit across.

Rows 3-21: Repeat Rows 1 and 2, 9 times; then repeat Row 1 once **more**.

Bind off all sts in **knit**, leaving a 15" (38 cm) length for sewing.

Thread yarn needle with end and sew Sides to Front and Back.

Thread yarn needle with Lt Green and sew Base to cast on edges of Front, Back and Sides. Stuff piece.

Thread yarn needle with end and weave through remaining sts; pull tightly and sew end of rows together. Using same yarn, sew Perch to Birdhouse below felt circle.

BIRD (Make 2)
BODY
TOP
With Lt Pink or Lt Blue and beginning at tail, cast on 2 sts.

Row 1 (Wrong side): Purl across.

Row 2: (Work invisible increase, K1) twice: 4 sts.

Row 3: Purl across.

Row 4: (K1, work invisible increase) twice, K2: 6 sts.

Row 5: Purl across.

Row 6: K2, work invisible increase, K1, work invisible increase, K3: 8 sts.

Row 7: Purl across.

Row 8: ★ Work invisible increase, K3, work invisible increase, K1; repeat from ★ once **more**: 12 sts.

Row 9: Purl across.

Row 10: ★ Work invisible increase, K5, work invisible increase, K1; repeat from ★ once **more**: 16 sts.

Row 11: Purl across.

Row 12: K7, work invisible increase, K1, work invisible increase, K8: 18 sts.

Row 13: Purl across.

Row 14: K8, work invisible increase, K1, work invisible increase, K9: 20 sts.

Row 15: Purl across.

Row 16: K2 tog, K7, work invisible increase, K1, work invisible increase, K8, K2 tog.

Row 17: Purl across.

Rows 18 and 19: Repeat Rows 16 and 17.

Row 20: K2 tog, K6, K2 tog twice, K6, K2 tog: 16 sts.

Row 21: Purl across.

Row 22: K2 tog, K4, K2 tog twice, K4, K2 tog: 12 sts.

Row 23: Purl across.

Row 24: K2 tog, K2, K2 tog twice, K2, K2 tog: 8 sts.

Bind off remaining sts in **purl**.

Fold piece in half across bound off edge with **wrong** side together, forming face. Sew across the 4 bound off sts.

BELLY
With Brown or Dk Brown and beginning at tail, cast on 2 sts.

Row 1 (Wrong side): Purl across.

Row 2: (Work invisible increase, K1) twice: 4 sts.

Row 3: Purl across.

Row 4: Knit across.

Row 5: Purl across.

Instructions continued on page 26.

Row 6 (Increase row)**:** Work invisible increase, knit across to last st, work invisible increase, K1: 6 sts.

Rows 7-10: Repeat Rows 3-6: 8 sts.

Row 11: Purl across.

Row 12: Knit across.

Rows 13-15: Repeat Rows 11 and 12 once, then repeat Row 11 once **more**.

Row 16 (Decrease row)**:** K2 tog, knit across to last 2 sts, K2 tog: 6 sts.

Row 17: Purl across.

Row 18: Knit across.

Row 19: Purl across.

Rows 20-23: Repeat Rows 16-19: 4 sts.

Row 24: K2 tog twice: 2 sts.

Row 25: P2 tog: one st.

Cut yarn and pull end through remaining st to finish off.

With **wrong** sides together, sew Top to Belly stuffing piece before closing (sew Lt Blue to Brown and Lt Pink to Dk Brown).

WING (Make 2)
With Brown or Dk Brown, cast on 8 sts.

Row 1 (Wrong side)**:** Purl across.

Row 2: ★ Work invisible increase, K3, work invisible increase, K1; repeat from ★ once **more**: 12 sts.

Row 3: Purl across.

Row 4: K2 tog, K2, K2 tog twice, K2, K2 tog: 8 sts.

Row 5: Purl across.

Row 6: K2 tog 4 times: 4 sts.

Cut yarn leaving a 12" (30.5 cm) length for sewing.

Thread yarn needle withyarn end and weave through remaining sts; pull tightly and sew end of rows together; then sew Wing to Body using photo as a guide for placement.

Trace beak pattern below and cut one piece from Brown or Dk Brown felt. Fold beak in half along line indicated. Using photo as a guide for placement, sew beak to face with sewing needle and thread.

Beak pattern

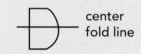

With Dk Brown yarn, add French knot eyes (*Fig. 9, page 111*).

A s bunnies go, Buster is a bit overindulged. His grandfather is a famous rabbit who makes Easter deliveries. The youngest bunny of several dozen, Buster finds himself at loose ends from time to time. Which means mischief tends to find him. On top of that, he's terribly forgetful. Also, he can't keep a secret to save his fuzzy little tail, and he misses school a lot of days because he wanders through the meadow instead of waiting at the bus stop. But he's no dumb bunny, so there's hope for him yet.

buster
BUNNY JR.

Instructions continued on page 28.

Finished Size: 8¹/₂" (21.5 cm) tall

MATERIALS
Medium Weight Yarn **4**
[6 ounces, 312 yards
(170 grams, 285 meters) per skein]:
   Off-White - 1 skein
   Pink - 1 skein
Straight knitting needles, size 4 (3.5 mm)
Polyester stuffing
6 mm Black doll eyes - 2
Yarn needle

Techniques used:
• Invisible increase
  (Fig. 1, page 110)
• K2 tog *(Fig. 3, page 110)*

HEAD AND BODY
With Off-White and beginning at top of Head, cast on 6 sts.

Row 1 (Wrong side)**:** Purl across.

Row 2 (Increase row)**:** (Work invisible increase, K1) across: 12 sts.

Rows 3 and 4: Repeat Rows 1 and 2: 24 sts.

Row 5: Purl across.

Row 6: Knit across.

Rows 7-13: Repeat Rows 5 and 6, 3 times; then repeat Row 5 once **more**.

Row 14 (neck)**:** K2 tog across: 12 sts.

Row 15: Purl across.

Row 16: (Work invisible increase, K1) across: 24 sts.

Row 17: Purl across.

Row 18: (Work invisible increase, K2) across: 36 sts.

Row 19: Purl across.

Row 20: Knit across.

Rows 21-35: Repeat Rows 19 and 20, 7 times; then repeat Row 19 once **more**.

Row 36: (K2 tog, K1) across: 24 sts.

Row 37: Purl across.

Row 38 (Decrease row)**:** K2 tog across: 12 sts.

Rows 39 and 40: Repeat Rows 37 and 38: 6 sts.

Cut Off-White leaving a 12" (30.5 cm) length for sewing.

Thread yarn needle with end and weave through remaining sts; pull tightly and sew end of rows together to neck.

Using photo as a guide for placement, page 27, attach eyes on Row 6.

Continue sewing seam, stuffing firmly as you go and gathering cast on edge to avoid leaving a hole.

With Pink and using photo as a guide, add satin stitch nose on Rows 7 and 8 *(Fig. 7, page 111)*.

ARM (Make 2)
With Off-White and beginning at shoulder, cast on 8 sts.

Row 1 (Wrong side)**:** Purl across.

Row 2: Knit across.

Rows 3-9: Repeat Rows 1 and 2, 3 times; then repeat Row 1 once **more**.

Row 10: K2 tog across: 4 sts.

Cut Off-White leaving a 12" (30.5 cm) length for sewing.

Thread yarn needle with end and weave through remaining sts; pull tightly and sew end of rows together. Sew Arms to each side of Body along Row 14.

LEG (Make 2)

With Off-White and beginning at Body edge, cast on 10 sts.

Row 1 (Wrong side): Purl across.

Row 2: Knit across.

Rows 3-9: Repeat Rows 1 and 2, 3 times; then repeat Row 1 once more.

Row 10: K4, work invisible increase, K1, work invisible increase, K5: 12 sts.

Row 11: Purl across.

Row 12: K5, work invisible increase, K1, work invisible increase, K6: 14 sts.

Row 13: Purl across.

Row 14: K5, K2 tog twice, K5: 12 sts.

Row 15: Purl across.

Row 16: K2 tog across: 6 sts.

Cut Off-White leaving a 12" (30.5 cm) length for sewing.

Thread yarn needle with end and weave through remaining sts; pull tightly and sew end of rows together stuffing lightly. Sew Legs to bottom of Body.

EAR (Make 2)

With Off-White and beginning at Head edge, cast on 6 sts.

Row 1 (Wrong side): Purl across.

Row 2: (Work invisible increase, K1) across: 12 sts.

Row 3: Purl across.

Row 4: Knit across.

Rows 5-13: Repeat Rows 3 and 4, 4 times; then repeat Row 3 once more.

Row 14: K2 tog, K2, K2 tog twice, K2, K2 tog: 8 sts.

Row 15: Purl across.

Row 16: K2 tog across: 4 sts.

Cut Off-White leaving a 12" (30.5 cm) length for sewing.

Thread yarn needle with end and weave through remaining sts; pull tightly and sew end of rows together. Sew Ears to top of Head.

TAIL

With Pink and beginning at Body edge, cast on 24 sts.

Row 1 (Wrong side): Purl across.

Row 2: Knit across.

Row 3: Purl across.

Row 4 (Decrease row): K2 tog across: 12 sts.

Rows 5 and 6: Repeat Rows 3 and 4: 6 sts.

Cut Pink leaving a 12" (30.5 cm) length for sewing.

Thread yarn needle with end and weave through remaining sts; pull tightly and sew end of rows together. Stuff lightly and sew Tail to bottom.

Young Miss Waddle finds herself in the distressing position of being a friend to Buster Bunny Jr. Always a good pal, Billie wants Buster to straighten up and pay attention to what's happening in his life, but she can't seem to get through to him. On the bright side, Billie has found an interest that's given her new confidence—open mike night at the local comedy club. She's too young for the circuit, but the regulars at the neighborhood spot like little Billie. As you may have guessed, her (slightly) exaggerated tales of Buster's misdoings really quack them up!

billie
WADDLE

Finished Size: 4" (10 cm) tall (seated)

MATERIALS

Medium Weight Yarn
[3¹/₂ ounces, 170 yards
(100 grams, 156 meters) per skein]:
    Yellow - 1 skein
    Orange - 1 skein
Straight knitting needles, size 4 (3.5 mm)
Polyester stuffing
6 mm Black doll eyes - 2
Yarn needle

Techniques used:
• Invisible increase
    (Fig. 1, page 110)
• K2 tog *(Fig. 3, page 110)*

HEAD AND BODY

With Yellow and beginning at top of Head, cast on 6 sts.

Row 1 (Wrong side)**:** Purl across.

Row 2 (Increase row)**:** (Work invisible increase, K1) across: 12 sts.

Rows 3 and 4: Repeat Rows 1 and 2: 24 sts.

Row 5: Purl across.

Row 6: Knit across.

Rows 7-13: Repeat Rows 5 and 6, 3 times; then repeat Row 5 once **more**.

Row 14 (neck)**:** K2 tog across: 12 sts.

Row 15: Purl across.

Row 16: (Work invisible increase, K1) across: 24 sts.

Row 17: Purl across.

Row 18: (Work invisible increase, K2) across: 36 sts.

Row 19: Purl across.

Row 20: Knit across.

Rows 21-33: Repeat Rows 19 and 20, 6 times; then repeat Row 19 once **more**.

Row 34: (K2 tog, K1) across: 24 sts.

Row 35: Purl across.

Row 36 (Decrease row)**:** K2 tog across: 12 sts.

Rows 37 and 38: Repeat Rows 35 and 36: 6 sts.

Cut Yellow leaving a 12" (30.5 cm) length for sewing.

Instructions continued on page 32.

Thread yarn needle with end and weave through remaining sts; pull tightly and sew end of rows together to neck.

Using photo as a guide for placement, attach eyes on Row 6.

Continue sewing seam, stuffing firmly as you go and gathering cast on edge to avoid leaving a hole.

BEAK
With Orange and beginning at face edge, cast on 12 sts.

Row 1 (Wrong side): Purl across.

Row 2: Knit across.

Row 3: Purl across.

Row 4: K2 tog across: 6 sts.

Cut Orange leaving a 10" (25.5 cm) length for sewing.

Thread yarn needle with end and weave through remaining sts; pull tightly and sew end of rows together. Using photo as a guide for placement, sew Beak to face.

WING (Make 2)
With Yellow, beginning at tip and leaving a long end for sewing, cast on 8 sts.

Row 1 (Wrong side): Purl across.

Row 2 (Increase row): Work invisible increase, knit across to last st, work invisible increase, K1: 10 sts.

Rows 3 and 4: Repeat Rows 1 and 2: 12 sts.

Row 5: Purl across.

Row 6: Knit across.

Row 7: Purl across.

Row 8 (Decrease row): K2 tog, knit across to last 2 sts, K2 tog: 10 sts.

Rows 9 and 10: Repeat Rows 7 and 8: 8 sts.

Bind off remaining sts in **purl**.

Fold Wing in half lengthwise with **wrong** side together. Thread yarn needle with beginning end and sew cast on edge together, then sew end of rows together. With seam toward the back, sew Wings to each side of Body along Row 14.

LEG (Make 2)
With Orange, beginning at Body edge and leaving a long end for sewing, cast on 10 sts.

Row 1 (Wrong side): Purl across.

Row 2: Knit across.

Rows 3-7: Repeat Rows 1 and 2 twice, then repeat Row 1 once **more**.

Row 8: ★ Work invisible increase, K4, work invisible increase, K1; repeat from ★ once **more**: 14 sts.

Row 9: Purl across.

Row 10: ★ Work invisible increase, K6, work invisible increase, K1; repeat from ★ once **more**: 18 sts.

Bind off all sts in **purl**.

Thread yarn needle with long end. Matching end of rows, sew Leg seam and across bind off edge.

Using photo as a guide for placement, sew Legs to Body.

N ow, just because he's wearing a ribbon, Hank doesn't want you to think he's soft. Well, his fleece is soft, but Hank isn't. He's all rough and tumble under that wool, a lamb looking forward to being a big, tough ram someday—maybe even the mascot for a pickup truck company or a football team. His mom has different ideas. She wants him to do something in the Arts or in Fashion—thus the ribbon. Well, adolescence is never easy. But Hank will learn to deal with all this fluffy stuff.

harold (hank)
LAMBSWOOL

Instructions continued on page 34.

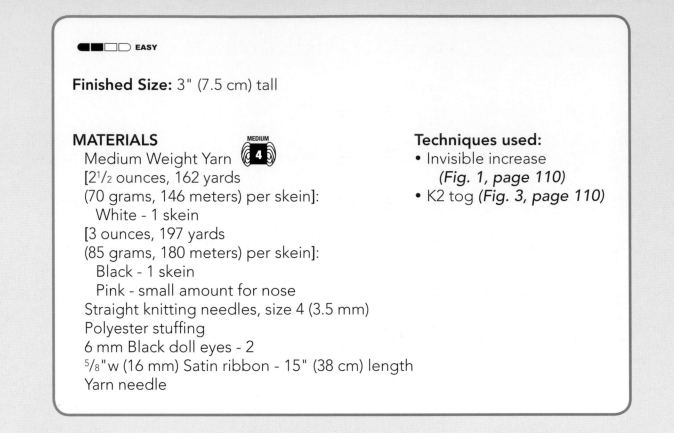

Finished Size: 3" (7.5 cm) tall

MATERIALS

Medium Weight Yarn
[2½ ounces, 162 yards
(70 grams, 146 meters) per skein]:
  White - 1 skein
[3 ounces, 197 yards
(85 grams, 180 meters) per skein]:
  Black - 1 skein
  Pink - small amount for nose
Straight knitting needles, size 4 (3.5 mm)
Polyester stuffing
6 mm Black doll eyes - 2
⅝"w (16 mm) Satin ribbon - 15" (38 cm) length
Yarn needle

Techniques used:
- Invisible increase
  (*Fig. 1, page 110*)
- K2 tog (*Fig. 3, page 110*)

BODY AND HEAD
With White and beginning at rear, cast on 6 sts.

Row 1 (Wrong side)**:** Knit across.

Row 2 (Increase row)**:** (Work invisible increase, K1) across: 12 sts.

Row 3: Knit across.

Rows 4 and 5: Repeat Rows 2 and 3: 24 sts.

Row 6: (Work invisible increase, K2) across: 36 sts.

Rows 7-23: Knit across.

Row 24: K2 tog 7 times, K8, K2 tog 7 times: 22 sts.

Row 25: Knit across.

Row 26 (neck)**:** K2 tog across: 11 sts.

Row 27: Knit across.

Row 28: K3, work invisible increase, (K1, work invisible increase) 4 times, K4: 16 sts.

Row 29: Knit across.

Row 30: K4, work invisible increase, (K1, work invisible increase) 7 times, K5: 24 sts.

Rows 31-35: Knit across.

Row 36: (K2 tog, K2) across; cut White leaving a long end for sewing: 18 sts.

Row 37: With Black, purl across.

Row 38: Knit across.

Row 39: Purl across.

Row 40: (K2 tog, K1) across: 12 sts.

Row 41: Purl across.

Rows 42 and 43: Repeat Rows 38 and 39.

Row 44: K2 tog across: 6 sts.

Cut Black leaving a 10" (25.5 cm) length for sewing.

Thread yarn needle with Black end and weave through remaining sts; pull tightly and sew end of rows together to neck with corresponding colors.

Using photo as a guide for placement, attach eyes on Row 38.

Continue sewing seam, stuffing firmly as you go and gathering cast on edge to avoid leaving a hole.

FOOT (Make 4)

With Black and beginning at Body edge, cast on 12 sts.

Row 1 (Wrong side): Purl across.

Row 2: Knit across.

Row 3: Purl across.

Row 4: K2 tog across: 6 sts.

Cut Black leaving a 10" (25.5 cm) length for sewing.

Thread yarn needle with end and weave through remaining sts; pull tightly and sew end of rows together. Stuff Foot; sew to Body using photo as a guide for placement.

EAR (Make 2)

With Black, and beginning at outer edge of Ear, cast on 6 sts.

Row 1 (Wrong side): Purl across.

Row 2: K2 tog, K2, K2 tog: 4 sts.

Row 3: K2 tog twice: 2 sts.

Row 4: K2 tog: one st.

Cut yarn leaving a long end for sewing and pull end through remaining st to finish off.

Thread yarn needle with end. Fold Ear in half and sew end of rows to Head, using photo as a guide for placement.

TAIL

With Black, cast on 20 sts.

Row 1: K2 tog across: 10 sts.

Bind off remaining sts in **knit**, leaving a long end for sewing.

Thread yarn needle with end. Curl Tail into curlicue and tack in place to hold shape; sew Tail to back of Body.

With Pink and using photo as a guide, add satin stitch nose *(Fig. 7, page 111)*.

Tie ribbon around neck.

the BIRDS and BEES

**Y**ou probably recognize these visitors to your garden. But have you ever thought about what they do at the end of a workday? Your backyard buddies recently formed the Sunny Vale Thespian Troupe! They're in production now for a summer run of *Romeo and Juliet*. Fred Leaper and Lindsay Ladybeetle have the title roles. Buzz Hover is Tybalt, while Oliver Who is the director and stage manager. Like most start-ups, the SV Thespians have had their rough moments. One night, "Romeo" skipped dinner before practice. He became so hungry that, in the midst of his first soliloquy, he almost made a meal of "Juliet." Lindsay is a tough ladybug, however, who refused to quit. "The play's the thing," she says. It also helps that Oliver is now stationed in the rafters, ready to swoop down on Fred if he so much as hears his tummy growl. Buzz Hover, well, he hovers nearby, stinger at ready. Fred's a bit jumpy these days.

ead-over-talons in love with the theatre ever since he attended summer stock two years ago, Oliver is in his element as a director of local plays. His great hope is that he'll be able to direct a show on Broadway one day. He's also a big fan of public television. His favorite show is the one where the famous acting school dean interviews notable persons in the film industry. He even speaks like the dean, with plenty of resonance and feeling. The Sunny Vale Thespians try hard not to laugh when Oliver gets carried away. He's been known to get so excited while shouting stage directions that he forgets he can fly. He's already fallen off the stage four times. It's a good thing that feathers make for a soft landing.

oliver
WHO

Finished Size: 10" (25.5 cm) tall

MATERIALS

Medium Weight Yarn
[3½ ounces, 170 yards
(100 grams, 156 meters) per skein]:
   Green - 1 skein
   Dk Pink - 1 skein
   Coral - 1 skein
   Yellow - 1 skein
   Blue - 1 skein
   Pink - 1 skein
   White - 1 skein
Straight knitting needles, size 4 (3.5 mm)
Yarn needle
Polyester stuffing
9 mm Black doll eyes - 2

Techniques used:
• Invisible increase (*Fig. 1, page 110*)
• K2 tog (*Fig. 3, page 110*)
• P2 tog (*Fig. 5, page 110*)

BODY
With Green and beginning at bottom, cast on 20 sts.

Row 1 (Wrong side)**:** Purl across.

Row 2 (Increase row)**:** Work invisible increase, knit across to last st, work invisible increase, K1: 22 sts.

Row 3: Purl across.

Rows 4-11: Repeat Rows 2 and 3, 4 times: 30 sts.

Row 12: Knit across.

Row 13: Purl across.

Rows 14-21: Repeat Rows 12 and 13, 4 times.

Row 22 (Decrease row)**:** K2 tog, knit across to last 2 sts, K2 tog: 28 sts.

Row 23: Purl across.

Rows 24-29: Repeat Rows 22 and 23, 3 times; at end of Row 29, cut Green: 22 sts.

Rows 30-33: With Dk Pink, repeat Rows 22 and 23 twice: 18 sts.

Row 34: Knit across.

Row 35: Purl across.

Instructions continued on page 40.

Row 36 (Increase row): Work invisible increase, knit across to last st, work invisible increase, K1: 20 sts.

Rows 37-44: Repeat Rows 35 and 36, 4 times: 28 sts.

Row 45: Purl across.

Row 46 (Decrease row): K2 tog, knit across to last 2 sts, K2 tog: 26 sts.

Row 47: Purl across.

Rows 48-55: Repeat Rows 46 and 47, 4 times: 18 sts.

Row 56: Knit across.

Row 57: Purl across.

Row 58: Work invisible increase, knit across to last st, work invisible increase, K1: 20 sts.

Row 59: Purl across; cut Dk Pink.

Row 60 (Increase row): With Green, work invisible increase, knit across to last st, work invisible increase, K1: 22 sts.

Row 61: Purl across.

Rows 62-69: Repeat Rows 60 and 61, 4 times: 30 sts.

Row 70: Knit across.

Row 71: Purl across.

Rows 72-79: Repeat Rows 70 and 71, 4 times.

Row 80 (Decrease row): K2 tog, knit across to last 2 sts, K2 tog: 28 sts.

Row 81: Purl across.

Rows 82-89: Repeat Rows 80 and 81, 4 times: 20 sts.

Bind off remaining sts in **knit**.

EYE (Make 2)
With White, cast on 6 sts.

Row 1 (Wrong side): Purl across.

Row 2 (Increase row): (Work invisible increase, K1) across: 12 sts.

Rows 3 and 4: Repeat Rows 1 and 2: 24 sts.

Bind off all sts in **purl**.

Sew end of rows together, forming a circle with a small hole in the center. Insert shank of doll eye through hole and set aside (do **not** fasten with washers).

BEAK
With Yellow and beginning at top, cast on 8 sts.

Row 1 (Wrong side): Purl across.

Row 2: K2 tog, K4, K2 tog: 6 sts.

Row 3: Purl across.

Row 4: K2 tog, K2, K2 tog: 4 sts.

Row 5: Purl across.

Row 6: K2 tog twice: 2 sts.

Row 7: P2 tog: one st.

Cut Yellow leaving a long end for sewing; pull end through last st.

Thread yarn needle with long end. Using photo as a guide for placement, page 38, sew Beak to Body, centering top of Beak along Row 30.

Attach eyes in stitches on Row 33, having center 8 sts between shanks of both eyes.

Fold Body in half widthwise. With colors and rows matching, sew side seam from the bottom up, using corresponding color, to the sixth Dk Pink row; then sew straight up to the fold, leaving the outer 5 or 6 sts free to form an ear.
Repeat on second side of Body.

With Green, sew bottom seam, stuffing Body firmly before closing.

LEG (Make 2)

With Yellow, beginning at foot and leaving a long end for sewing, cast on 36 sts.

Row 1 (Wrong side): Purl across.

Row 2: K2 tog, K5, (K2 tog twice, K5) 3 times, K2 tog: 28 sts.

Row 3: Purl across.

Row 4: K2 tog, K3, (K2 tog twice, K3) 3 times, K2 tog: 20 sts.

Row 5: Purl across.

Row 6: K2 tog, K1, (K2 tog twice, K1) 3 times, K2 tog: 12 sts.

Row 7: Purl across; cut Yellow.

Row 8: With Blue, knit across.

Row 9: Purl across; drop Blue.

Row 10: With Pink, knit across.

Row 11: Purl across; drop Pink.

Rows 12-27: Repeat Rows 8-11, 4 times; at end of Row 27, cut Pink.

Row 28: With Blue, knit across.

Row 29: Purl across.

Bind off remaining sts in **knit**.

Sew end of rows together using corresponding color for each section, stuffing Leg before closing; sew opening at bottom of foot closed.

Sew Legs to bottom edge of Body.

WING (Make 2)

With Coral, beginning at tip and leaving a long end for sewing, cast on 8 sts.

Row 1 (Wrong side): Purl across.

Row 2 (Increase row): Work invisible increase, knit across to last st, work invisible increase, K1: 10 sts.

Row 3: Purl across.

Rows 4-7: Repeat Rows 2 and 3 twice: 14 sts.

Row 8: Knit across.

Row 9: Purl across.

Row 10 (Decrease row): K2 tog, knit across to last 2 sts, K2 tog: 12 sts.

Rows 11-14: Repeat Rows 9 and 10 twice: 8 sts.

Bind off remaining sts in **purl**.

Thread yarn needle with beginning end and sew seam, matching end of rows.

With rounded edge toward the front, sew Wings to side of Body near color change.

R eally, you can't go around wearing yellow-and-black stripes all your life and not become known as an independent sort. Buzz has taken his role as Tybalt to heart. Acting as Juliet's belligerent cousin in the play, he's also ended up being Lindsay's bodyguard against "that frog"— as he refers to Fred. Buzz got bored a long time ago with his old job of visiting flowers. He's had a lot of jobs in recent months and says the acting gig is just time-filler until he figures out what he really wants to do.

buzz
HOVER

Finished Size: 13" (33 cm) tall

MATERIALS

Medium Weight Yarn
[3¹/₂ ounces, 170 yards
(100 grams, 156 meters) per skein]:
  Black - 1 skein
  White - 1 skein
  Yellow - 1 skein
  Dk Red - small amount for mouth
Straight knitting needles, size 4 (3.5 mm)
Yarn needle
Polyester stuffing
9 mm Black doll eyes - 2

Techniques used:
• Invisible increase
  (Fig. 1, page 110)
• K2 tog *(Fig. 3, page 110)*
• P2 tog *(Fig. 5, page 110)*

BODY

With Black and beginning at bottom, cast on 20 sts.

Row 1 (Wrong side)**:** Purl across.

Row 2: Work invisible increase, knit across to last st, work invisible increase, K1: 22 sts.

Row 3: Purl across; drop Black.

Row 4 (Increase row)**:** With Yellow, work invisible increase, knit across to last st, work invisible increase, K1: 24 sts.

Row 5: Purl across.

Rows 6 and 7: Repeat Rows 4 and 5; at end of Row 7, drop Yellow: 26 sts.

Row 8 (Increase row)**:** With Black, work invisible increase, knit across to last st, work invisible increase, K1: 28 sts.

Row 9: Purl across.

Rows 10 and 11: Repeat Rows 8 and 9; at end of Row 11, drop Black: 30 sts.

Row 12: With Yellow, knit across.

Row 13: Purl across.

Row 14: Knit across.

Row 15: Purl across; drop Yellow.

Row 16: With Black, knit across.

Row 17: Purl across.

Row 18: Knit across.

Row 19: Purl across; drop Black.

Instructions continued on page 44.

Rows 20-27: Repeat Rows 12-19.

Row 28 (Decrease row): With Yellow, K2 tog, knit across to last 2 sts, K2 tog: 28 sts.

Row 29: Purl across.

Rows 30 and 31: Repeat Rows 28 and 29; at end of Row 31, drop Yellow: 26 sts.

Row 32 (Decrease row): With Black, K2 tog, knit across to last 2 sts, K2 tog: 24 sts.

Row 33: Purl across.

Rows 34 and 35: Repeat Rows 32 and 33; at end of Row 35, cut Black: 22 sts.

Row 36 (Increase row): With Yellow, work invisible increase, knit across to last st, work invisible increase, K1: 24 sts.

Row 37: Purl across.

Rows 38 and 39: Repeat Rows 36 and 37: 26 sts.

Row 40: Knit across.

Row 41: Purl across.

Rows 42 and 43: Repeat Rows 40 and 41.

Row 44 (Decrease row): K2 tog, knit across to last 2 sts, K2 tog: 24 sts.

Row 45: Purl across.

Rows 46-49: Repeat Rows 44 and 45 twice: 20 sts.

Row 50 (Increase row): Work invisible increase, knit across to last st, work invisible increase, K1: 22 sts.

Row 51: Purl across.

Rows 52-55: Repeat Rows 50 and 51 twice: 26 sts.

Rows 56-63: Repeat Rows 40-47; at end of Row 63, drop Yellow: 22 sts.

Row 64 (Increase row): With Black, work invisible increase, knit across to last st, work invisible increase, K1: 24 sts.

Row 65: Purl across.

Rows 66 and 67: Repeat Rows 64 and 65; at end of Row 67, drop Black: 26 sts.

Row 68 (Increase row): With Yellow, work invisible increase, knit across to last st, work invisible increase, K1: 28 sts.

Row 69: Purl across.

Rows 70 and 71: Repeat Rows 68 and 69; at end of Row 71, drop Yellow: 30 sts.

Row 72: With Black, knit across.

Row 73: Purl across.

Row 74: Knit across.

Row 75: Purl across; drop Black.

Row 76: With Yellow, knit across.

Row 77: Purl across.

Row 78: Knit across.

Row 79: Purl across; drop Yellow.

Rows 80-89: Repeat Rows 72-79 once, then repeat Rows 72 and 73 once **more**.

Row 90: K2 tog, knit across to last 2 sts, K2 tog: 28 sts.

Row 91: Purl across; drop Black.

Row 92 (Decrease row): With Yellow, K2 tog, knit across to last 2 sts, K2 tog: 26 sts.

Row 93: Purl across.

Rows 94 and 95: Repeat Rows 92 and 93; at end of Row 95, cut Yellow: 24 sts.

Row 96: With Black, K2 tog, knit across to last 2 sts, K2 tog: 22 sts.

Row 97: Purl across.

Row 98: K2 tog, knit across to last 2 sts, K2 tog: 20 sts.

Bind off remaining sts in **purl**.

Attach eyes in stitches on Row 42 having center 8 sts between shanks of both eyes.

With Dk Red, add straight stitch mouth *(Fig. 8, page 111)*.

Fold Body in half widthwise. With colors and rows matching, sew side and bottom seams with corresponding color, stuffing Body firmly before closing.

LEG (Make 2)
With Black and beginning at top, cast on 12 sts.

Row 1: Purl across.

Row 2 (Right side): Knit across.

Rows 3-25: Repeat Rows 1 and 2, 11 times; then repeat Row 1 once **more**; at end of Row 25, cut Black leaving a 12" (30.5 cm) length for sewing.

Row 26: With Yellow, (work invisible increase, K1) across: 24 sts.

Row 27: Purl across.

Row 28: Knit across.

Rows 29-33: Repeat Rows 27 and 28 twice, then repeat Row 27 once **more**.

Row 34: K2 tog across: 12 sts.

Row 35: P2 tog across: 6 sts.

Cut Yellow leaving a 6" (15 cm) length for sewing.

Thread yarn needle with Yellow end and weave through remaining sts; pull tightly and sew end of rows together using corresponding color for each section, stuffing Leg before closing.

Sew Legs to bottom edge of Body.

Instructions continued on page 46.

ARM (Make 2)

With Black and beginning at shoulder, cast on 8 sts.

Row 1: Purl across.

Row 2 (Right side)**:** Knit across.

Rows 3-19: Repeat Rows 1 and 2, 8 times; then repeat Row 1 once **more**; at end of Row 19, cut Black leaving a 12" (30.5 cm) length for sewing.

Row 20: With Yellow, (work invisible increase, K1) across: 16 sts.

Row 21: Knit across.

Row 22: Purl across.

Rows 23-25: Repeat Rows 21 and 22 once, then repeat Row 21 once **more**.

Row 26: K2 tog across: 8 sts.

Row 27: P2 tog across: 4 sts.

Cut Yellow leaving a 6" (15 cm) length for sewing.

Thread yarn needle with Yellow end and weave through remaining sts; pull tightly and sew end of rows together using corresponding color for each section, stuffing Arm before closing.

Sew Arms to each side, along top of last Black stripe.

WING (Make 2)

With White and beginning at Body edge, cast on 24 sts.

Row 1 (Wrong side)**:** Purl across.

Row 2 (Increase row)**:** ★ Work invisible increase, K 11, work invisible increase, K1; repeat from ★ once **more**: 28 sts.

Rows 3-8: Repeat Rows 1 and 2, 3 times: 40 sts.

Row 9: Purl across.

Row 10: Knit across.

Rows 11-17: Repeat Rows 9 and 10, 3 times; then repeat Row 9 once **more**.

Row 18: K2 tog across: 20 sts.

Row 19: Purl across.

Row 20: K2 tog across: 10 sts.

Row 21: P2 tog across: 5 sts.

Cut White leaving a 12" (30.5 cm) length for sewing.

Thread yarn needle with end and weave through remaining sts; pull tightly and sew end of rows together.

Sew each Wing to side of Body behind Arm, sewing across top 4 stripes.

ANTENNA (Make 2)

With Black and beginning at head edge, cast on 5 sts.

Row 1 (Wrong side)**:** Purl across.

Row 2: Knit across.

Rows 3-7: Repeat Rows 1 and 2 twice, then repeat Row 1 once **more**; at end of Row 7, cut Black.

Row 8: With Yellow, (work invisible increase, K1) across: 10 sts.

Rows 9-11: Repeat Rows 1 and 2 once, then repeat Row 1 once **more**.

Row 12: K2 tog across: 5 sts.

Cut Yellow leaving a 10" (25.5 cm) length for sewing.

Thread yarn needle with end and weave through remaining sts; pull tightly and sew end of rows together using corresponding color for each section, stuffing Antenna before closing.

Sew each Antenna to top of Head.

Poor frazzled Fred. Who knew a little thing like skipping a meal would cause such a big fuss? He was greatly relieved to know that he didn't actually harm Lindsay. It's just that he was starving when he saw her fly up into Juliet's balcony. Anything that flies is naturally going to get a frog's attention. So now Fred hops onto the stage with his eyes closed. If he doesn't see Lindsay fly, he won't be tempted to catch her. Sure, it's an odd way to start the first romantic scene, but it beats eating the leading lady—not to mention getting attacked by a melodramatic owl and an itinerate bee.

fred
LEAPER

Instructions begin on page 48.

Finished Size:
10" (25.5 cm) tall

MATERIALS

Medium Weight Yarn
[3½ ounces, 170 yards
(100 grams, 156 meters)
per skein]:
   Lt Green - 1 skein
   Green - 1 skein
   Dk Green - 1 skein
   White - 1 skein
   Dk Red - small amount
   for mouth
Straight knitting needles,
   size 4 (3.5 mm)
Yarn needle
Polyester stuffing
9 mm Black doll eyes - 2

Techniques used:
- Invisible increase
  (Fig. 1, page 110)
- K2 tog *(Fig. 3, page 110)*

BODY

With Lt Green and beginning at bottom, cast on 20 sts.

Row 1 (Wrong side)**:** Purl across.

Row 2 (Increase row)**:** Work invisible increase, knit across to last st, work invisible increase, K1: 22 sts.

Row 3: Purl across.

Rows 4-9: Repeat Rows 2 and 3, 3 times: 28 sts.

Row 10: Knit across.

Row 11: Purl across.

Rows 12-23: Repeat Rows 10 and 11, 6 times.

Row 24 (Decrease row)**:** K2 tog, knit across to last 2 sts, K2 tog: 26 sts.

Row 25: Purl across.

Rows 26-33: Repeat Rows 24 and 25, 4 times: 18 sts.

Row 34: Knit across.

Row 35: Purl across.

Row 36 (Increase row)**:** Work invisible increase, knit across to last st, work invisible increase, K1: 20 sts.

Row 37: Purl across.

Rows 38 and 39: Repeat Rows 36 and 37: 22 sts.

Row 40: Knit across.

Row 41: Purl across.

Row 42 (Decrease row)**:** K2 tog, knit across to last 2 sts, K2 tog: 20 sts.

Row 43: Purl across.

Rows 44 and 45: Repeat Rows 42 and 43: 18 sts.

Rows 46-55: Repeat Rows 36-45.

Row 56: Knit across.

Row 57: Purl across.

Row 58 (Increase row)**:** Work invisible increase, knit across to last st, work invisible increase, K1: 20 sts.

Row 59: Purl across.

Rows 60-67: Repeat Rows 58 and 59, 4 times: 28 sts.

Row 68: Knit across.

Row 69: Purl across.

Rows 70-81: Repeat Rows 68 and 69, 6 times.

Row 82 (Decrease row)**:** K2 tog, knit across to last 2 sts, K2 tog: 26 sts.

Row 83: Purl across.

Rows 84-89: Repeat Rows 82 and 83, 3 times: 20 sts.

Bind off remaining sts in **knit**.

EYE (Make 2)

With White, cast on 6 sts.

Row 1 (Wrong side)**:** Purl across.

Row 2 (Increase row)**:** (Work invisible increase, K1) across: 12 sts.

Rows 3 and 4: Repeat Rows 1 and 2: 24 sts.

Bind off all sts in **purl**.

Sew end of rows together, forming a circle with a small hole in the center. Insert shank of doll eye through hole and set aside (do **not** fasten with washers).

TUMMY

With Green and beginning at top, cast on 14 sts.

Row 1 (Wrong side): Purl across.

Row 2 (Increase row): Work invisible increase, knit across to last st, work invisible increase, K1: 16 sts.

Rows 3-8: Repeat Rows 1 and 2, 3 times: 22 sts.

Row 9: Purl across.

Row 10: Knit across.

Rows 11-20: Repeat Rows 9 and 10, 5 times.

Row 21: Purl across.

Row 22 (Decrease row): K2 tog, knit across to last 2 sts, K2 tog: 20 sts.

Rows 23-28: Repeat Rows 21 and 22, 3 times: 14 sts.

Bind off remaining sts in **purl**.

Thread yarn needle with a 15" (38 cm) length of Green. With **wrong** side of Tummy and **right** side of Body together, centering Tummy and having bound off edge of Tummy even with top of sts on Row 1 of Body, sew Tummy to Body.

Attach eyes in stitches on Row 41, having center 8 sts between shanks of both eyes.

With Dk Red and using photo as a guide for placement, add straight stitch mouth *(Fig. 8, page 111)*.

Fold Body in half widthwise and sew sides and bottom seam, stuffing Body before closing.

LEG (Make 2)

With Dk Green and beginning at foot, cast on 28 sts.

Row 1 (Wrong side): Purl across.

Row 2: K2 tog, K3, (K2 tog twice, K3) 3 times, K2 tog: 20 sts.

Row 3: Purl across.

Row 4: K2 tog, K1, (K2 tog twice, K1) 3 times, K2 tog: 12 sts.

Row 5: Purl across.

Row 6: Knit across.

Instructions continued on page 50.

Row 7: Purl across; cut Dk Green.

Row 8: With Green, knit across.

Row 9: Purl across; drop Green.

Row 10: With Lt Green, knit across.

Row 11: Purl across; drop Lt Green.

Rows 12-27: Repeat Rows 8-11, 4 times; at end of Row 27, cut Lt Green.

Row 28: With Green, knit across.

Row 29: Purl across.

Bind off remaining sts in **knit**, leaving a long end for sewing.

Thread yarn needle with end and sew end of rows together using corresponding color for each section, stuffing Leg before closing.

Sew Legs to bottom edge of Body.

ARM (Make 2)
With Dk Green and beginning at hand, cast on 24 sts.

Row 1 (Wrong side)**:** Purl across.

Row 2: K2 tog, K2, (K2 tog twice, K2) 3 times, K2 tog: 16 sts.

Row 3: Purl across.

Row 4: K2 tog across: 8 sts.

Row 5: Purl across.

Row 6: Knit across.

Row 7: Purl across; cut Dk Green.

Row 8: With Green, knit across.

Row 9: Purl across; drop Green.

Row 10: With Lt Green, knit across.

Row 11: Purl across; drop Lt Green.

Rows 12-15: Repeat Rows 8-11; at end of Row 15, cut Lt Green.

Row 16: With Green, knit across.

Row 17: Purl across.

Bind off remaining sts in **knit**, leaving a long end for sewing.

Thread yarn needle with end and sew end of rows together using corresponding color for each section, stuffing Arm before closing.

Using photo as a guide for placement, sew Arms to each side of Body.

When she isn't acting, Lindsay's life is that of a regular ladybug—eating aphids and flying from one plant to another. One new thing, however, is her interest in opera. Someone told her she has a fantastic singing voice. She signed up for classes a few weeks ago, and now she sings as she wings about the garden. It's good thing she does so well with her role as Juliet. Something tells us she won't be appearing on any recording labels in the near future.

lindsay
LADYBEETLE

Instructions begin on page 52.

Finished Size: 13" (33 cm) tall

MATERIALS
Medium Weight Yarn
[3¹/₂ ounces, 170 yards
(100 grams, 156 meters) per skein]:
   Black - 1 skein
   Red - 1 skein
   White - 1 skein
Straight knitting needles, size 4 (3.5 mm)
Yarn needle
Polyester stuffing
9 mm Black doll eyes - 2

Techniques used:
• Invisible increase *(Fig. 1, page 110)*
• K2 tog *(Fig. 3, page 110)*
• P2 tog *(Fig. 5, page 110)*

BODY
With Black and beginning at bottom, cast on 18 sts.

Row 1 (Wrong side)**:** Purl across.

Row 2 (Increase row)**:** Work invisible increase, knit across to last st, work invisible increase, K1: 20 sts.

Row 3: Purl across.

Rows 4-13: Repeat Rows 2 and 3, 5 times: 30 sts.

Row 14: Knit across.

Row 15: Purl across.

Rows 16-23: Repeat Rows 14 and 15, 4 times.

Row 24 (Decrease row)**:** K2 tog, knit across to last 2 sts, K2 tog: 28 sts.

Row 25: Purl across.

Rows 26-33: Repeat Rows 24 and 25, 4 times: 20 sts.

Row 34: Knit across.

Row 35: Purl across.

Row 36 (Increase row)**:** Work invisible increase, knit across to last st, work invisible increase, K1: 22 sts.

Row 37: Purl across.

Rows 38 and 39: Repeat Rows 36 and 37: 24 sts.

Row 40: Knit across.

Row 41: Purl across.

Rows 42 and 43: Repeat Rows 40 and 41.

Row 44 (Decrease row)**:** K2 tog, knit across to last 2 sts, K2 tog: 22 sts.

Row 45: Purl across.

Rows 46-49: Repeat Rows 44 and 45 twice: 18 sts.

Row 50: Knit across.

Row 51: Purl across.

Row 52 (Increase row)**:** Work invisible increase, knit across to last st, work invisible increase, K1: 20 sts.

Row 53: Purl across.

Rows 54-57: Repeat Rows 52 and 53 twice: 24 sts.

Row 58: Knit across.

Row 59: Purl across.

Rows 60 and 61: Repeat Rows 58 and 59.

Row 62 (Decrease row)**:** K2 tog, knit across to last 2 sts, K2 tog: 22 sts.

Row 63: Purl across.

Rows 64 and 65: Repeat Rows 62 and 63: 20 sts.

Row 66: Knit across.

Row 67: Purl across.

Row 68 (Increase row)**:** Work invisible increase, knit across to last st, work invisible increase, K1: 22 sts.

Row 69: Purl across.

Rows 70-77: Repeat Rows 68 and 69, 4 times: 30 sts.

Row 78: Knit across.

Row 79: Purl across.

Rows 80-87: Repeat Rows 78 and 79, 4 times.

Row 88 (Decrease row)**:** K2 tog, knit across to last 2 sts, K2 tog: 28 sts.

Row 89: Purl across.

Rows 90-99: Repeat Rows 88 and 89, 5 times: 18 sts.

Bind off remaining sts in **knit**.

EYE (Make 2)
With White, cast on 8 sts.

Row 1 (Wrong side)**:** Purl across.

Row 2 (Increase row)**:** (Work invisible increase, K1) across: 16 sts.

Bind off all sts in **purl**, leaving a long end for sewing.

Thread yarn needle with long end and sew end of rows together, forming a circle with a small hole in the center. Insert shank of doll eye through hole and set aside (do **not** fasten with washers).

Attach eyes in stitches on Row 42, having center 6 sts between shanks of both eyes. With Red and using photo as a guide for placement, page 51, add mouth using straight stitches (*Fig. 8, page 111*).

Fold Body in half widthwise. With Black, sew side seams and bottom, stuffing Body firmly before closing.

Instructions continued on page 54.

LEG (Make 2)

With Black and beginning at top of Leg, cast on 12 sts.

Row 1 (Wrong side): Purl across.

Row 2: Knit across.

Rows 3-22: Repeat Rows 1 and 2, 10 times.

Row 23: Purl across; cut Black.

Row 24: With Red, (work invisible increase, K1) across: 24 sts.

Rows 25-31: Repeat Rows 1 and 2, 3 times; then repeat Row 1 once **more**.

Row 32: K2 tog across: 12 sts.

Row 33: P2 tog across: 6 sts.

Cut Red leaving a 12" (30.5 cm) length for sewing.

Thread yarn needle with end and weave through remaining sts; pull tightly and sew end of rows together with corresponding color for each section. Stuff Leg and using photo as a guide for placement, sew to bottom of Body.

ARM (Make 2)

With Black and beginning at shoulder, cast on 8 sts.

Row 1 (Wrong side): Purl across.

Row 2: Knit across.

Rows 3-14: Repeat Rows 1 and 2, 6 times.

Row 15: Purl across; cut Black.

Row 16: With Red, (work invisible increase, K1) across: 16 sts.

Rows 17-21: Repeat Rows 1 and 2 twice, then repeat Row 1 once **more**.

Row 22: K2 tog across: 8 sts.

Row 23: P2 tog across: 4 sts.

Cut Red leaving a 12" (30.5 cm) length for sewing.

Thread yarn needle with end and weave through remaining sts; pull tightly and sew end of rows together with corresponding color for each section. Stuff Arm and using photo as a guide for placement, sew to each side of Body at neck.

WING (Make 2)

With Red and beginning at top, cast on 22 sts.

Row 1 (Wrong side): Purl across.

Row 2: K9, work invisible increase, (K1, work invisible increase) 3 times, K 10: 26 sts.

Row 3: Purl across.

Row 4: K2 tog, K9, work invisible increase, (K1, work invisible increase) 3 times, K 10, K2 tog: 28 sts.

Row 5: Purl across.

Row 6: K 12, work invisible increase, (K1, work invisible increase) 3 times, K 13: 32 sts.

Row 7: Purl across.

Row 8: K2 tog, K 13, work invisible increase, K1, work invisible increase, K 14, K2 tog.

Row 9: Purl across.

Row 10: Knit across.

Row 11: Purl across.

Row 12 (Decrease row): K2 tog, knit across to last 2 sts, K2 tog: 30 sts.

Rows 13-19: Repeat Rows 9-12 once, then repeat Rows 9-11 once **more**: 28 sts.

Row 20: K2 tog, K 10, K2 tog twice, K 10, K2 tog: 24 sts.

Rows 21-23: Repeat Rows 9-11.

Row 24: K2 tog, K8, K2 tog twice, K8, K2 tog: 20 sts.

Row 25: Purl across.

Row 26: K8, K2 tog twice, K8: 18 sts.

Row 27: Purl across.

Row 28: K2 tog, K5, K2 tog twice, K5, K2 tog: 14 sts.

Row 29: Purl across.

Row 30: K5, K2 tog twice, K5: 12 sts.

Row 31: Purl across.

Row 32: K2 tog, K2, K2 tog twice, K2, K2 tog: 8 sts.

Row 33: Purl across.

Row 34: K2, K2 tog twice, K2: 6 sts.

Row 35: Purl across.

Row 36: K2 tog across: 3 sts.

Cut Red leaving a 12" (30.5 cm) length for sewing.

Thread yarn needle with end and weave through remaining sts; pull tightly and sew end of rows together.

LARGE SPOT (Make 2)
With Black, cast on 6 sts.

Row 1 (Wrong side)**:** Purl across.

Row 2: (Work invisible increase, K1) across: 12 sts.

Rows 3 and 4: Repeat Rows 1 and 2: 24 sts.

Bind off all sts in **purl**, leaving a long end for sewing.

Thread yarn needle with end and sew end of rows together; weave yarn through cast on sts and gather to close hole in the center.

SMALL SPOT (Make 2)
With Black, cast on 8 sts.

Row 1 (Wrong side)**:** Purl across.

Row 2: (Work invisible increase, K1) across: 16 sts.

Bind off all sts in **purl**, leaving a long end for sewing.

Thread yarn needle with end and sew end of rows together; weave yarn through cast on sts and gather to close hole in the center.

Using photo as a guide for placement, sew one Large and one Small Spot to each Wing.

Thread yarn needle with a 15" (38 cm) length of Red. Using photo as a guide for placement, sew Wings to front of Body.

ANTENNA (Make 2)
With Black, cast on 5 sts.

Row 1 (Wrong side)**:** Purl across.

Row 2: Knit across.

Rows 3-7: Repeat Rows 1 and 2 twice, then repeat Row 1 once **more**; at end of Row 7, cut Black.

Row 8: With Red, (work invisible increase, K1) across: 10 sts.

Rows 9-11: Repeat Rows 1 and 2 once, then repeat Row 1 once **more**.

Row 12: K2 tog across: 5 sts.

Cut Red leaving a 10" (25.5 cm) length for sewing.

Thread yarn needle with end and weave through remaining sts; pull tightly and sew end of rows together using corresponding color for each section, stuffing Antenna before closing.

Sew each Antenna to top of Head.

forest FRIENDS

he Forest Friends are glad you were able to attend this meeting. They're working to promote awareness for the conservation of the Big-Cap Oak Tree. Never heard of the BCO? It gets its name from its big capped acorns. These trees are being systematically cut down and taken to a flooring factory. The Forest Friends want everyone to know that BCO wood doesn't differ from any other oak wood, so floors should be made from common oaks. Also, the friends want you to know that if the BCOs vanish, the White-Spotted Mushrooms (WSMs) are the next to go. That's because they only grow under BCO Trees. And that brings us to the real problem: The WSM is a staple in the diets of the Forest Friends. Which means the next time you see these little folk, they may be joining you for meals. It's up to you. Help them save the Big-Cap Oaks, or add six more chairs around the dinner table. Oh, by the way, the Forest Friends want you to know they're really fond of corn on the cob.

She gives a hoot. She really does. Odessa has been sounding the alarm for the environment for several years. It's tough to watch the tall timber disappear. All the wonderful hollow trees are disappearing along with them. And now the rare BCO is endangered! Goodness, it makes her head spin around. That's why she rallied the Forest Friends for this meeting. She wants them to invite the city folk to come see the trees for themselves. It might be the only way to save the Big-Capped Oaks.

odessa OWL

Finished Size: 3³/₄" (9.5 cm) tall

MATERIALS
  Medium Weight Yarn
  [6 ounces, 312 yards
  (170 grams, 285 meters) per skein]:
   Dk Brown - 1 skein
   Brown 1 skein
Straight knitting needles, size 4 (3.5 mm)
Felt - small amounts of White, Tan,
  Dk Brown and Gold
Polyester stuffing
9 mm Black doll eyes - 2
Sewing needle and matching thread
Yarn needle

Techniques used:
• Invisible increase (*Fig. 1, page 110*)
• K2 tog (*Fig. 3, page 110*)

BODY AND HEAD
With Dk Brown and beginning at bottom, cast on 6 sts.

Row 1 (Wrong side)**:** Purl across.

Row 2 (Increase row)**:** (Work invisible increase, K1) across: 12 sts.

Row 3: Purl across.

Rows 4-7: Repeat Rows 2 and 3 twice: 48 sts.

Row 8: Knit across.

Row 9: Purl across.

Rows 10-25: Repeat Rows 8 and 9, 8 times.

Row 26: (K2 tog, K6) across: 42 sts.

Row 27: Purl across.

Row 28: (K2 tog, K5) across: 36 sts.

Row 29: Purl across.

Row 30: (K2 tog, K4) across: 30 sts.

Row 31: Purl across.

Row 32: (K2 tog, K3) across: 24 sts.

Row 33: Purl across.

Row 34: K2 tog across: 12 sts.

Rows 35 and 36: Repeat Rows 33 and 34: 6 sts.

Instructions continued on page 60.

Cut Dk Brown leaving a 12" (30.5 cm) length for sewing.

Thread yarn needle with end and weave through remaining sts; pull tightly and sew end of rows together halfway.

Trace patterns below. Cut 2 large circles from White, 2 small circles from Tan and one beak from Gold. Cut 2 outer ears from Dk Brown and 2 inner ears from Tan.

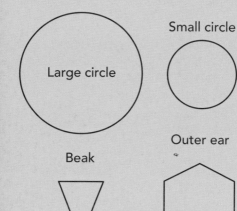

Using photo as a guide for placement, page 58:
Arrange small circle on top of large circle and insert shank of doll eye through both pieces; attach eyes to Head along Row 30.
With needle and matching thread, sew beak between eyes.

Finish sewing seam, stuffing piece firmly as you go and gathering cast on edge to avoid leaving a hole.

Arrange inner ear on top of outer ear. Folding piece in half at base, sew ears to top of Head with matching thread.

WING (Make 2)
With Brown and beginning at tip, cast on 6 sts.

Row 1 (Wrong side): Purl across.

Row 2: (Work invisible increase, K1) across: 12 sts.

Row 3: Purl across; cut Brown leaving a long end.

Row 4: With Dk Brown, (work invisible increase, K1) across: 24 sts.

Row 5: Purl across.

Row 6: Knit across.

Rows 7-11: Repeat Rows 5 and 6 twice, then repeat Row 5 once **more**.

Row 12: K2 tog across: 12 sts.

Bind off remaining sts in **purl**, leaving a 10" (25.5 cm) length for sewing.

Thread yarn needle with end and sew end of rows together using matching yarn and gathering cast on edge to avoid leaving a hole.

Flatten Wing having seam at center back. Using photo as a guide for placement, sew Wings to Body.

H

oratio is nervous about the idea of urbanites visiting the forest. He's heard about the pet hedgehog trend. He has a cozy retreat in the underbrush just outside the city park, so he'd rather not have to give that up for a bunch of ooey-cooey baby talk and the chance to live in a box in someone's living room. No thanks. Horatio is a wild hedgehog, and he wants to keep it that way. Now, if you do have corn on the cob, he maybe could negotiate a part-time venture. On a trial basis, you see.

horatio
HEDGEHOG

Instructions begin on page 62.

■■□□ **EASY**

Finished Size: 2³/₄" (7 cm) tall

MATERIALS
Medium Weight Yarn
[3 ounces, 157 yards
(90 grams, 144 meters) per skein]:
  Tan - 1 skein
  Dk Brown - small amount for nose
Bulky Weight Novelty Yarn
[1.75 ounces, 64 yards
(50 grams, 58 meters) per skein]:
  Dk Brown - 1 skein
Straight knitting needles, size 4 (3.5 mm)
Felt - small amount of Dk Brown
Polyester stuffing
6 mm Black doll eyes - 2
Sewing needle and matching thread
Yarn needle

Techniques used:
• Invisible increase (*Fig. 1, page 110*)
• K2 tog (*Fig. 3, page 110*)
• Slip 1 as if to **knit**, K1, PSSO (*Fig. 4, page 110*)

BODY AND HEAD
With Tan and beginning at rear, cast on 6 sts.

Row 1 (Wrong side): Purl across.

Row 2 (Increase row): (Work invisible increase, K1) across: 12 sts.

Rows 3-6: Repeat Rows 1 and 2 twice: 48 sts.

Row 7: Purl across.

Row 8: Knit across.

Rows 9-21: Repeat Rows 7 and 8, 6 times; then repeat Row 7 once **more**.

Row 22: K2 tog across: 24 sts.

Row 23: Purl across.

Row 24: ★ Slip 1, K1, PSSO, K8, K2 tog; repeat from ★ once **more**: 20 sts.

Row 25: Purl across.

Row 26: ★ Slip 1, K1, PSSO, K6, K2 tog; repeat from ★ once **more**: 16 sts.

Row 27: Purl across.

Row 28: ★ Slip 1, K1, PSSO, K4, K2 tog; repeat from ★ once **more**: 12 sts.

Row 29: Purl across.

Row 30: ★ Slip 1, K1, PSSO, K2, K2 tog; repeat from ★ once **more**: 8 sts.

Row 31: Purl across; cut Tan leaving a 15" (38 cm) length for sewing.

Row 32 (nose): With Dk Brown, (slip 1, K1, PSSO, K2 tog) twice: 4 sts.

Cut Dk Brown leaving a long end for sewing.

Thread yarn needle with end and weave through remaining sts; pull tightly and sew end of rows together halfway, using corresponding color.

Using photo as a guide for placement, page 61, attach eyes on Row 23.

Continue sewing seam, stuffing firmly as you go and gathering cast on edge to avoid leaving a hole.

FUR

With 2 strands of Dk Brown novelty yarn held together and beginning at rear, cast on 3 sts.

Row 1 (Wrong side): Knit across.

Row 2 (Increase row): (Work invisible increase, K1) across: 6 sts.

Rows 3-6: Repeat Rows 1 and 2 twice: 24 sts.

Rows 7-21: Knit across.

Row 22: K2 tog across: 12 sts.

Bind off remaining sts in **knit**.

Pin bound off edge of Fur along Row 25 of Body and Head and cast on edge at back of Body and Head. Sew Fur in place.

Trace pattern below. Cut 2 ears from Dk Brown felt. Using photo as a guide, sew ears to Head at edge of Fur.

Ear

63

Cinda's usually a perky kind of gal who likes nothing better than getting all fluffed up for a cause. But she's not quite herself at the moment. She ate a bad mushroom and became a bit tipsy. If she makes a comment about you needing lots and lots of makeup, please don't take it personally. She thinks everyone looks like a zombie today. Got to be careful about old mushrooms.

cinda
SQUIRREL

Finished Size: 5³/₄" (14.5 cm) tall

MATERIAL
Medium Weight Yarn
[6 ounces, 312 yards
(170 grams, 285 meters) per skein]:
    Brown - 1 skein
    Dk Brown - small amount for nose
Bulky Weight Novelty Yarn
[1.75 ounces, 64 yards
(50 grams, 58 meters) per skein]:
    Rust - 1 skein
Straight knitting needles, size 4 (3.5 mm)
Felt - small amounts of Tan and Dk Brown
Polyester stuffing
6 mm Black doll eyes - 2
Sewing needle and matching thread
Yarn needle

Techniques used:
• Invisible increase (*Fig. 1, page 110*)
• Knit increase (*Figs. 2a & b, page 110*)
• K2 tog (*Fig. 3, page 110*)
• Slip 1 as if to **knit**, K1, PSSO (*Fig. 4, page 110*)

BODY AND HEAD
With Brown and beginning at bottom, cast on 6 sts.

Row 1 (Wrong side): Purl across.

Row 2 (Increase row): (Work invisible increase, K1) across: 12 sts

Rows 3-6: Repeat Rows 1 and 2 twice: 48 sts.

Row 7: Purl across.

Row 8: Knit across.

Rows 9-27: Repeat Rows 7 and 8, 9 times; then repeat Row 7 once more.

Row 28: K 10, slip 1, K1, PSSO, K2 tog, K 20, slip 1, K1, PSSO, K2 tog, K 10: 44 sts.

Row 29: Purl across.

Row 30: K9, slip 1, K1, PSSO, K2 tog, K 18, slip 1, K1, PSSO, K2 tog, K9: 40 sts.

Row 31: Purl across.

Row 32: K8, slip 1, K1, PSSO, K2 tog, K 16, slip 1, K1, PSSO, K2 tog, K8: 36 sts.

Row 33: Purl across.

Instructions continued on page 66.

Row 34 (neck): K2 tog across: 18 sts.

Row 35: Purl across.

Row 36: (Work invisible increase, K1) across: 36 sts.

Row 37: Purl across.

Row 38: Knit across.

Row 39: Purl across.

Row 40: K7, [work invisible increase, (K1, work invisible increase) 3 times (beginning of cheek)], K 15, [work invisible increase, (K1, work invisible increase) 3 times (beginning of cheek)], K8: 44 sts.

Rows 41-43: Repeat Rows 37-39.

Row 44: K7, [(slip 1, K1, PSSO) twice, K2 tog twice (end of cheek)], K5, [slip 1, K1, PSSO, K2 tog (nose)], K5, [(slip 1, K1, PSSO) twice, K2 tog twice (end of cheek)], K7: 34 sts.

Row 45: Purl across.

Row 46: K 15, slip 1, K1, PSSO, K2 tog, K 15: 32 sts.

Row 47: Purl across.

Row 48: K 14, slip 1, K1, PSSO, K2 tog, K 14: 30 sts.

Row 49: Purl across.

Row 50: K 13, slip 1, K1, PSSO, K2 tog, K 13: 28 sts.

Row 51: Purl across.

Row 52 (Decrease row): K2 tog across: 14 sts.

Rows 53 and 54: Repeat Rows 51 and 52: 7 sts.

Cut Brown leaving a 15" (38 cm) length for sewing.

Thread yarn needle with end and weave through remaining sts; pull tightly and sew end of rows together halfway.

Using photo as a guide for placement, page 64, attach eyes on Row 47.

Continue sewing seam, stuffing firmly as you go and gathering cast on edge to avoid leaving a hole.

With Dk Brown and using photo as a guide, add satin stitch nose on Row 46 *(Fig. 7, page 111)*.

Trace patterns below. Cut 2 outer ears from Dk Brown felt and 2 inner ears from Tan.

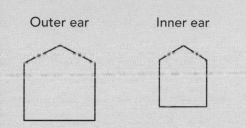

Outer ear   Inner ear

Arrange inner ear on top of outer ear. Using photo as a guide, sew ears to top of Head with matching thread.

FOOT (Make 2)
With Brown and beginning at back of Foot, cast on 12 sts.

Row 1 (Wrong side)**:** Purl across.

Row 2: Knit across.

Rows 3-9: Repeat Rows 1 and 2, 3 times; then repeat Row 1 once **more**.

Row 10: K2 tog across: 6 sts.

Cut Brown leaving a 12" (30.5 cm) length for sewing.

Thread yarn needle with end and weave through remaining sts; pull tightly and sew end of rows together. Stuff the end of Foot lightly. Flatten cast on edge with seam at center bottom and sew to bottom of Body.

ARM (Make 2)
With Brown and beginning at shoulder, cast on 10 sts.

Row 1 (Wrong side)**:** Purl across.

Row 2: Knit across.

Rows 3-5: Repeat Rows 1 and 2 once, then repeat Row 1 once **more**.

Row 6: K2 tog across: 5 sts.

Cut Brown leaving a 12" (30.5 cm) length for sewing.

Thread yarn needle with end and weave through remaining sts; pull tightly and sew end of rows together. Flatten cast on edge with seam at center bottom and sew to each side of Body along Row 34.

TAIL
With 2 strands of Rust held together and beginning at bottom, cast on 12 sts.

Row 1 (Wrong side)**:** Knit across.

Row 2: Work knit increases across: 24 sts.

Rows 3-41: Knit across.

Row 42: K2 tog across: 12 sts.

Row 43: Knit across.

Row 44: K2 tog across: 6 sts.

Cut Rust leaving a 15" (38 cm) length for sewing.

Thread yarn needle with end and weave through remaining sts; pull tightly and sew end of rows together stuffing Tail lightly. Flatten Tail with seam at center back.
With Brown, sew cast on edge to bottom of Body. Tack Tail to center of back with Brown.

N ow, just because Cinda got a fermented mushroom, don't be thinking the WSMs are a bad fungus. They really are delicious and a great source of minerals. Woodland gnomes developed them a long time ago to look like dangerous mushrooms so that mushroom poachers would stay away. Unless you're eating WSMs at the end of the season and you didn't check them for freshness, they're perfectly fine. Yes, there's nothing prettier than a whole patch of WSMs growing in the wild! If you happen to be hiking in the woods, keep an eye out for them. If you're lucky, you may also spot the pointed red hat of a gnome as he works nearby.

white-spotted MUSHROOM

Finished Size: 3¹/₂" (9 cm) tall

MATERIALS
Medium Weight Yarn
[3¹/₂ ounces, 170 yards
(100 grams, 156 meters) per skein]:
  Dk Red - 1 skein
  White - 1 skein
Straight knitting needles, size 4 (3.5 mm)
Yarn needle
Polyester stuffing

Techniques used:
• Invisible increase
   (*Fig. 1, page 110*)
• K2 tog (*Fig. 3, page 110*)
• P2 tog (*Fig. 5, page 110*)

STEM

With White and beginning at bottom, cast on 5 sts.

Row 1 (Wrong side): Purl across.

Row 2 (Increase row): (Work invisible increase, K1) across: 10 sts.

Rows 3 and 4: Repeat Rows 1 and 2: 20 sts.

Row 5: Knit across.

Row 6: (K3, P1) across.

Row 7: (K1, P3) across.

Rows 8-16: Repeat Rows 6 and 7, 4 times; then repeat Row 6 once **more**.

Row 17: Purl across; cut White leaving a 10" (25.5 cm) end for sewing.

CAP

Row 1 (Increase row): With Dk Red, (work invisible increase, K1) across: 30 sts.

Row 2: Knit across.

Row 3: (Work invisible increase, K2) across: 45 sts.

Rows 4 and 5: Knit across.

Row 6: Purl across.

Rows 7-16: Repeat Rows 5 and 6, 5 times.

Row 17 (Decrease row): (K2 tog, K1) across: 30 sts.

Row 18: Purl across.

Rows 19 and 20: Repeat Rows 17 and 18: 20 sts.

Row 21: K2 tog across: 10 sts.

Row 22: P2 tog across: 5 sts.

Cut Dk Red leaving a 10" (25.5 cm) length for sewing.

Thread yarn needle with end and weave through remaining sts; pull tightly and sew end of rows together with corresponding color, stuffing firmly as you go and gathering cast on edge to avoid leaving a hole.

LARGE SPOT

With White, cast on 8 sts.

Row 1 (Wrong side): Purl across.

Row 2: (Work invisible increase, K1) across: 16 sts.

Row 3: Purl across.

Row 4: (Work invisible increase, K2) across: 24 sts.

Bind off all sts in **purl**, leaving a long end for sewing.

Thread yarn needle with end and sew end of rows together; weave yarn through cast on sts and gather to close hole in the center.

SMALL SPOT

Work same as Large Spot through Row 2: 16 sts.

Bind off all sts in **purl**, leaving a long end for sewing.

Thread yarn needle with end and sew end of rows together; weave yarn through cast on sts and gather to close hole in the center.

Using photo as a guide for placement, sew Spots to Cap.

She doesn't mind taking her turn at pulling Horatio's wagon, but it riles her a bit that she thinks it's funny to yell "Mush!" Pippa Mouse left her sixteen children at home with a sitter, so she's eager to get this little gathering over with. Sure, you would think she'd be happy to get away for a while, but have you heard what sitters charge for just one kid these days? It's outrageous.

pippa
MOUSE

Finished Size: 4⅛" (10.5 cm) tall

MATERIALS

Medium Weight Yarn
[5 ounces, 260 yards
(141 grams, 238 meters) per skein]:
 Brown - 1 skein
 Pink - small amount for nose
Straight knitting needles, size 4 (3.5 mm)
Felt - small amounts of Brown and Pink
Polyester stuffing
6 mm Black doll eyes - 2
Sewing needle and matching thread
Yarn needle

Techniques used:

• Invisible increase
 (Fig. 1, page 110)
• K2 tog *(Fig. 3, page 110)*
• P2 tog *(Fig. 5, page 110)*
• Slip 1 as if to **knit**, K1, PSSO
 (Fig. 4, page 110)

BODY AND HEAD

With Brown and beginning at bottom, cast on 6 sts.

Row 1 (Wrong side): Purl across.

Row 2 (Increase row): (Work invisible increase, K1) across. 12 sts.

Rows 3 and 4: Repeat Rows 1 and 2: 24 sts.

Row 5: Purl across.

Row 6: Knit across.

Rows 7-17: Repeat Rows 5 and 6, 5 times; then repeat Row 5 once **more**.

Row 18: K4, slip 1, K1, PSSO, K2 tog, K8, slip 1, K1, PSSO, K2 tog, K4: 20 sts.

Row 19: Purl across.

Row 20: K3, slip 1, K1, PSSO, K2 tog, K6, slip 1, K1, PSSO, K2 tog, K3: 16 sts.

Row 21: Purl across.

Row 22 (neck): (K2 tog, K2) across: 12 sts.

Row 23: Purl across.

Row 24: (Work invisible increase, K1) across: 24 sts.

Row 25: Purl across.

Row 26: K 11, [work invisible increase, K1, work invisible increase (to begin forming nose)], K 12: 26 sts.

Row 27: Purl across.

Row 28: K 12, [work invisible increase, K1, work invisible increase (to finish forming nose)], K 13: 28 sts.

Row 29: Purl across.

Row 30: K 12, slip 1, K1, PSSO, K2 tog, K 12: 26 sts.

Row 31: Purl across.

Row 32: K 11, slip 1, K1, PSSO, K2 tog, K 11: 24 sts.

Row 33: Purl across.

Row 34 (Decrease row): K2 tog across: 12 sts.

Rows 35 and 36: Repeat Rows 33 and 34: 6 sts.

Cut Brown leaving a 15" (38 cm) length for sewing.

Instructions continued on page 72.

Thread yarn needle with end and weave through remaining sts; pull tightly and sew end of rows together halfway.

Using photo as a guide for placement, page 70, attach eyes on Row 30.

Continue sewing seam, stuffing firmly as you go and gathering cast on edge to avoid leaving a hole.

With Pink and using photo as a guide, add satin stitch nose on Rows 28 and 29 (*Fig. 7, page 111*).

Trace patterns below. Cut 2 outer ears from Brown felt and 2 inner ears from Pink.

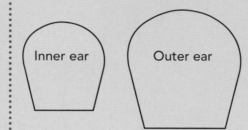

Inner ear   Outer ear

Arrange inner ear on top of outer ear. Folding piece in half at base, sew ears to top of Head with matching thread.

LIMB (Make 2 for Arms and 2 for Feet)
With Brown, cast on 8 sts.

Row 1 (Wrong side)**:** Purl across.

Row 2: Knit across.

Rows 3-7: Repeat Rows 1 and 2 twice, then repeat Row 1 once **more.**

Row 8: K2 tog across: 4 sts.

Cut Brown leaving a 12" (30.5 cm) length for sewing.

Thread yarn needle with end and weave through remaining sts; pull tightly and sew end of rows together.

For Feet, flatten piece with seam at center of bottom, then sew cast on edge to bottom of Body.

For Arms, flatten piece with seam at center of inside, then sew cast on edge to each side of Body along Row 22.

To make tail, attach a 4" (10 cm) length of Brown yarn to back of Mouse. Tie a knot in the end to prevent fraying.

These European gnomes have only been living nearby for a couple of centuries, so their accents are still quite charming. It's pleasant to hear them speak, don't you think? They're attending this neighborhood meeting for a slightly different reason than that of their friends'. The truth is, gnomes are excellent farmers, so they can grow another variety of mushrooms if the WSMs die out. However, no matter how you look at it, there's no way to grow corn in the forest. That's why Erik and Gunnar are hoping you'll decide to help protect the mushroom habitat—it could be the start of good trade relations. Maybe you'll be willing to exchange a few ears of corn for a basket of mushrooms now and then? And maybe you could throw in a stick of butter? You know you like mushrooms on your pizza. How about mushroom gravy? Give it some thought.

erik &
GUNNAR

Instructions begin on page 74.

Finished Size: 9" (23 cm) tall

MATERIALS (for one Gnome)
  Medium Weight Yarn **MEDIUM 4**
  [3 ounces, 197 yards
  (85 grams, 180 meters) per skein]:
    Green or Blue - 1 ball
    Off-White - 1 ball
    Black - 1 ball
    Red - 1 ball
  [2½ ounces, 162 yards
  (70 grams, 146 meters) per skein]:
    White - 1 ball
  Straight knitting needles, size 4 (3.5 mm)
  Yarn needle
  Polyester stuffing
  Gold belt buckle (optional)
  Blush (optional)

Techniques used:
• Invisible increase (*Fig. 1, page 110*)
• K2 tog (*Fig. 3, page 110*)
• P2 tog (*Fig. 5, page 110*)
• Slip 1 as if to **knit**, K1, PSSO (*Fig. 4, page 110*)
• K3 tog (*Fig. 6, page 110*)

BOTTOM
With Green or Blue, cast on 14 sts.

Row 1 (Wrong side): Purl across.

Row 2 (Increase row): Work invisible increase, knit across to last st, work invisible increase, K1: 16 sts.

Row 3: Purl across.

Rows 4 and 5: Repeat Rows 2 and 3: 18 sts.

Row 6: Knit across.

Row 7: Purl across.

Row 8 (Decrease row): Slip 1, K1, PSSO, knit across to last 2 sts, K2 tog: 16 sts.

Row 9: Purl across.

Rows 10 and 11: Repeat Rows 8 and 9: 14 sts.

Bind off all sts in **knit**.

BODY
With Green or Blue, cast on 42 sts.

Row 1 (Wrong side): Purl across.

Row 2: Knit across.

Rows 3-11: Repeat Rows 1 and 2, 4 times; then repeat Row 1 once **more**.

Row 12: K8, K2 tog, K2, slip 1, K1, PSSO, K 14, K2 tog, K2, slip 1, K1, PSSO, K8: 38 sts.

Row 13: Purl across.

Row 14: K7, K2 tog, K2, slip 1, K1, PSSO, K 12, K2 tog, K2, slip 1, K1, PSSO, K7: 34 sts.

Row 15: Purl across.

Row 16: K6, K2 tog, K2, slip 1, K1, PSSO, K 10, K2 tog, K2, slip 1, K1, PSSO, K6: 30 sts.

Row 17: Purl across.

Row 18: K5, K2 tog, K2, slip 1, K1, PSSO, K8, K2 tog, K2, slip 1, K1, PSSO, K5: 26 sts.

Row 19: Purl across; cut yarn leaving a 12" (30.5 cm) length for sewing.

HEAD
Row 1: With Off-White, (K1, K2 tog) across to last 2 sts, K2: 18 sts.

Row 2: Purl across.

Row 3: K1, (work invisible increase, K2) across to last 3 sts, work invisible increase, K3: 26 sts.

Row 4: Purl across.

Row 5: K2, (work invisible increase, K3) across: 34 sts.

Row 6: Purl across.

Row 7: K 15, work invisible increase, (K1, work invisible increase) 3 times, K 16: 38 sts.

Row 8: Purl across.

Row 9: K 17, K2 tog, slip 1, K1, PSSO, K 17: 36 sts.

Row 10: Purl across.

Row 11: K 16, K2 tog, slip 1, K1, PSSO, K 16: 34 sts.

Row 12: Purl across.

Row 13: Knit across.

Row 14: Purl across.

Row 15 (Decrease row)**:** K1, K2 tog across to last st, K1: 18 sts.

Rows 16 and 17: Repeat Rows 14 and 15: 10 sts.

Row 18: P2 tog across: 5 sts.

Cut Off-White leaving a 10" (25.5 cm) length for sewing.

Thread yarn needle with end and weave through remaining sts.

Instructions continued on page 76.

EAR (Make 2)

With Off-White, cast on 6 sts.

Row 1 (Wrong side): Purl across.

Row 2: Work invisible increase, K4, K2 tog.

Row 3: Purl across.

Row 4: Knit across.

Row 5: Purl across.

Row 6: Slip 1, K1, PSSO, K3, work invisible increase, K1.

Row 7: Purl across.

Bind off all sts **knit**.

HAT

With Red, cast on 30 sts.

Row 1 (Wrong side): Purl across.

Row 2: Knit across.

Rows 3-9: Repeat Rows 1 and 2, 3 times; then repeat Row 1 once **more**.

Row 10: (Slip 1, K1, PSSO, K6, K2 tog) across: 24 sts.

Row 11: Purl across.

Row 12: (Slip 1, K1, PSSO, K4, K2 tog) across: 18 sts.

Row 13: Purl across.

Row 14: (Slip 1, K1, PSSO, K2, K2 tog) across: 12 sts.

Row 15: Purl across.

Row 16: (Slip 1, K1, PSSO, K2 tog) across: 6 sts.

Row 17: Purl across.

Row 18: K2 tog across: 3 sts.

Row 19: Purl across.

Row 20: K3 tog; cut yarn leaving a 12" (30.5 cm) length for sewing: one st.

Pull end through remaining st to finish off. Thread yarn needle with end and sew end of rows together to form a cone; stuff Hat.

ARM (Make 2)
With Green or Blue, cast on 12 sts.

Row 1 (Wrong side): Purl across.

Row 2: Knit across.

Rows 3-7: Repeat Rows 1 and 2 twice, then repeat Row 1 once more.

Cut yarn leaving a 10" (25.5 cm) length for sewing.

Row 8: With Off-White, knit across.

Row 9: Purl across.

Row 10: K5, work invisible increase, K1, work invisible increase, K6: 14 sts.

Row 11: Purl across.

Row 12: K5, work invisible increase, K3, work invisible increase, K6: 16 sts.

Row 13: Purl across.

Row 14: K6, bind off next 4 sts, K5: 12 sts.

Row 15: Purl across sts on each side of bound off sts.

Row 16: (Slip 1, K1, PSSO, K2, K2 tog) twice: 8 sts.

Row 17: Purl across.

Row 18: (Slip 1, K1, PSSO, K2 tog) twice: 4 sts.

Bind off all sts in **purl**, leaving a long end for sewing.

Fold in half and sew end of rows together using corresponding color for each section; stuff Arm.

BEARD
With White and beginning at top, cast on 8 sts.

Row 1: Slip 1 as if to **purl**, knit across.

Row 2 (Increase row): Work invisible increase, knit across to last st, work invisible increase: 10 sts.

Rows 3 and 4: Repeat Rows 1 and 2: 12 sts.

Rows 5-12: Slip 1 as if to **purl**, knit across.

Rows 13-21: Slip 1, K1, PSSO, knit across: 3 sts.

Row 22: Slip 1, K1, PSSO, K1: 2 sts.

Row 23: Slip 1, K1, PSSO; cut yarn and pull end through remaining st to finish off: one st.

MUSTACHE (Make 2)
With White, cast on 3 sts.

Row 1: Slip 1 as if to **purl**, knit across.

Row 2 (Increase row): Work invisible increase, knit across: 4 sts.

Rows 3 and 4: Repeat Rows 1 and 2: 5 sts.

Rows 5-7: Slip 1 as if to **purl**, knit across.

Rows 8 and 9: Slip 1, K1, PSSO, knit across: 3 sts.

Row 10: Slip 1, K1, PSSO, K1: 2 sts.

Row 11: Slip 1, K1, PSSO, cut yarn and pull end through remaining st to finish off: one st.

BOOT (Make 2)
With Black, beginning at bottom and leaving a long end for sewing, cast on 20 sts.

Row 1 (Wrong side): Purl across.

Row 2: Knit across.

Row 3: Purl across.

Row 4: K7, K2 tog, K2, slip 1, K1, PSSO, K7: 18 sts.

Row 5: Purl across.

Instructions continued on page 78.

Row 6: K6, K2 tog, K2, slip 1, K1, PSSO, K6: 16 sts.

Row 7: Purl across.

Row 8: K5, K2 tog, K2, slip 1, K1, PSSO, K5: 14 sts.

Rows 9-11: Repeat Rows 1-3.

Rows 12 and 13: Knit across.

Bind off remaining sts in **knit**, leaving a 10" (25.5 cm) length for sewing.

Thread yarn needle with end.

Fold piece in half lengthwise and sew end of rows together; then sew cast on edge together.

BELT (Optional)
With Black, cast on 4 sts.

Row 1: WYB slip 1 as if to **purl**, K1, P1, K1.

Row 2: WYF slip 1 as if to **purl**, P1, K1, P1.

Repeat Rows 1 and 2 until Belt measures approximately 10½" (26.5 cm).

Bind off all sts in pattern.

Sew end of Belt to buckle.

FINISHING

Using photo as a guide, page 73: With Black, add eyes using French knots (*Fig. 9, page 111*). If desired, add White eyebrows using straight stitch (*Fig. 8, page 111*).

Sew Beard above Body color change; add Red satin stitches above center of beard for mouth (*Fig. 7, page 111*); sew Mustache above mouth.

Sew back seam for Head and Body to cast on edge.

Sew Hat to Head above eyebrows and eyes. Add White French Knots at base of Hat for Hair if desired (*see photo, page 75*).

Attach Arms along color change at shoulders; attach Ears to face above Arms. Stuff Body firmly. Align the Bottom with the cast on edge of the Body and sew in place, adding additional stuffing if desired. Stuff Boots (you may use polyfill beads if desired); sew Boots to Bottom.

Fasten Belt around waist if desired.

D arn cute, isn't it? We bet you've never seen such a healthy nut before! Hopefully, the Forest Friends will be able to stop the tree harvest. In the meantime, you can help out by storing some of these impressive acorns in your home. Once the ban on cutting is official, you'll surely want to help cultivate as many Big-Capped Oak Trees as possible. It's the responsible thing to do.

big-capped
ACORN

Instructions begin on page 80.

Finished Size: 2¹/₂" (6.5 cm) tall

MATERIALS

Medium Weight Yarn
[6 ounces, 312 yards
(170 grams, 285 meters) per skein]:
  Dk Brown - 1 skein
[3 ounces, 157 yards
(100 grams, 144 meters) per skein]:
  Tan - 1 skein
Straight knitting needles, size 4 (3.5 mm)
Polyester stuffing
Yarn needle

Techniques used:
• Invisible increase (*Fig. 1, page 110*)
• Knit increase (*Figs. 2a & b, page 110*)
• K2 tog (*Fig. 3, page 110*)

NUT
With Tan and beginning at top, cast on 6 sts.

Row 1 (Wrong side): Purl across.

Row 2 (Increase row): (Work invisible increase, K1) across: 12 sts.

Row 3: Purl across.

Rows 4 and 5: Repeat Rows 2 and 3: 24 sts.

Row 6: Knit across.

Row 7: Purl across.

Rows 8-15: Repeat Rows 6 and 7, 4 times.

Row 16: (K2 tog, K2) across: 18 sts.

Row 17: Purl across.

Row 18: (K2 tog, K1) across: 12 sts.

Row 19: Purl across.

Row 20: K2 tog across: 6 sts.

Cut Tan leaving a 12" (30.5 cm) length for sewing.

Thread yarn needle with end and weave through remaining sts; pull tightly and sew end of rows together, stuffing piece firmly as you go and gathering cast on edge to avoid leaving a hole.

CAP

With Dk Brown and beginning at bottom, cast on 24 sts.

Row 1 (Wrong side): Purl across.

Row 2: (Work knit increase, K3) across: 30 sts.

Row 3: Purl across.

Row 4: (Work knit increase, K4) across: 36 sts.

Row 5: Purl across.

Row 6: Knit across.

Row 7: Purl across.

Row 8: (K2 tog, K4) across: 30 sts.

Row 9: Purl across.

Row 10: (K2 tog, K3) across: 24 sts.

Row 11: Purl across.

Row 12: (K2 tog, K2) across: 18 sts.

Row 13: Purl across.

Row 14: (K2 tog, K1) across: 12 sts.

Row 15: Purl across.

Row 16: K2 tog across: 6 sts.

Cut Dk Brown leaving a 12" (30.5 cm) length for sewing.

Thread yarn needle with end and weave through remaining sts; pull tightly and secure end. Leaving a $1/2$" (1.25 cm) loop at top, sew end of rows together.

Put Cap on top of Nut.

bean TRIO

**I**t's easy to spot a group of tourists, isn't it? What's different about the Bean Trio is the fact that they're all packed and ready to go—but can't agree on where they're going. The camera buff, Harold Hopper, wants to snap some shots of Yellowstone. The fellow with the map, Boyce Bruin, is thinking Canadian wilderness. But the third friend, Thaddeus Trotter, is a bit phobic about wolves—which leaves out both choices. These Bean Town boys will be like this for a while. In the meantime, let's hope the taxi doesn't leave without them.

Uh oh. Shutterbug alert! Harold loves his Nikon. And his Canon. In fact, there's not a camera model he hasn't owned at one time or another. Still shots, video, he does it all. If you've ever watched one of those home video shows—the kind where the amateur camera operator keeps filming while Great-Grandma falls into the deep end of the swimming pool—that's Harold. His life only happens through the lens.

harold
HOPPER

Finished Size: 12" (30.5 cm) tall

MATERIALS

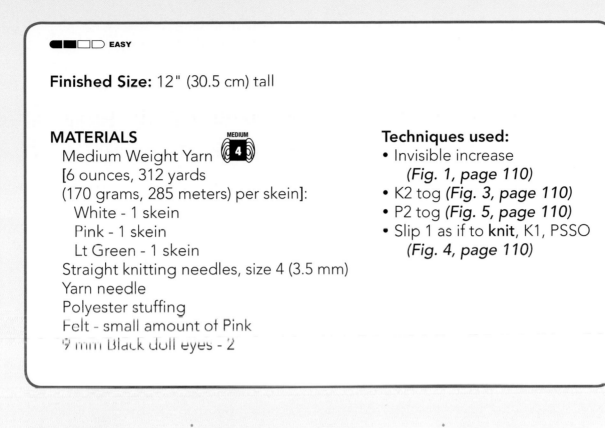

Medium Weight Yarn **4**
[6 ounces, 312 yards
(170 grams, 285 meters) per skein]:
  White - 1 skein
  Pink - 1 skein
  Lt Green - 1 skein
Straight knitting needles, size 4 (3.5 mm)
Yarn needle
Polyester stuffing
Felt - small amount of Pink
9 mm Black doll eyes - 2

Techniques used:
- Invisible increase
  (Fig. 1, page 110)
- K2 tog *(Fig. 3, page 110)*
- P2 tog *(Fig. 5, page 110)*
- Slip 1 as if to **knit**, K1, PSSO
  (Fig. 4, page 110)

BODY AND HEAD

With White and beginning at bottom of Body, cast on 6 sts.

Row 1 (Wrong side)**:** Purl across.

Row 2 (Increase row)**:**
(Work invisible increase, K1) across: 12 sts.

Row 3: Purl across.

Rows 4-7: Repeat Rows 2 and 3 twice: 48 sts.

Row 8: Knit across.

Row 9: Purl across.

Rows 10-21: Repeat Rows 8 and 9, 6 times.

Cut White.

Row 22: With Lt Green, knit across.

Row 23: Purl across; drop Lt Green.

Row 24: With Pink, knit across.

Row 25: Purl across.

Rows 26 and 27: Repeat Rows 24 and 25; at end of Row 27, drop Pink.

Rows 28-33: Repeat Rows 22-27; at end of Row 33, cut Pink.

Row 34: With Lt Green, knit across.

Row 35: Purl across; cut Lt Green.

Row 36: With White, knit across.

Row 37: Purl across.

Rows 38-53: Repeat Rows 36 and 37, 8 times.

Row 54 (Decrease row)**:**
K2 tog across: 24 sts.

Row 55: Purl across.

Rows 56-58: Repeat Rows 54 and 55 once, then repeat Row 54 once **more**: 6 sts.

Cut White leaving a 15" (38 cm) length for sewing.

Thread yarn needle with end and weave through remaining sts; pull tightly and sew end of rows together to Lt Green.

Instructions continued on page 86.

Trace flower pattern below and cut 2 flowers from pink felt.

Flower pattern

Insert shank of doll eye through center of each felt flower. Using photo as a guide, page 84, attach eyes to face. Using corresponding colors, finish sewing seam, stuffing firmly as you go.

With Pink and referring to photo as a guide for placement, add satin stitch nose (*Fig. 7, page 111*).

EAR (Make 2)
With White and beginning at bottom of Ear, cast on 16 sts.

Row 1 (Wrong side): Purl across.

Row 2: Knit across.

Rows 3-13: Repeat Rows 1 and 2, 5 times; then repeat Row 1 once **more**.

Row 14: (Slip 1, K1, PSSO, K4, K2 tog) twice: 12 sts.

Row 15: Purl across.

Row 16: (Slip 1, K1, PSSO, K2, K2 tog) twice: 8 sts.

Row 17: Purl across.

Row 18: K2 tog across: 4 sts.

Cut yarn leaving a 15" (38 cm) length for sewing.

Thread yarn needle with end and weave through remaining sts; pull tightly and sew end of rows together; do not stuff.

At bottom of Ear, fold flattened piece in half with seam at edge and sew together. Using photo as a guide for placement, sew Ears to Head.

ARM (Make 2)
With White, leaving a long end for sewing and beginning at hand, cast on 4 sts.

Row 1 (Wrong side): Purl across.

Row 2 (Increase row): (Work invisible increase, K1) across: 8 sts.

Row 3: Purl across.

Rows 4 and 5: Repeat Rows 2 and 3: 16 sts.

Row 6: Knit across.

Row 7: Purl across.

Rows 8-11: Repeat Rows 5 and 6 twice; at end of Row 11, cut White.

Row 12: With Lt Green, knit across.

Row 13: Purl across; drop Lt Green.

Row 14: With Pink, knit across.

Row 15: Purl across.

Rows 16 and 17: Repeat Rows 13 and 14; at end of Row 17, drop Pink.

Rows 18-23: Repeat Rows 12-17; at end of Row 23, cut Pink.

Row 24: With Lt Green, knit across.

Bind off all sts in **purl**.

Thread yarn needle with long end and sew end of rows together using corresponding colors. Stuff Arm, then flatten opening with seam at center of bottom. Using photo as a guide, sew to Body along Lt Green.

LEG (Make 2)
With White and beginning at top of Leg, cast on 16 sts.

Row 1: Purl across.

Row 2 (Right side): Knit across.

Rows 3-19: Repeat Rows 1 and 2, 8 times; then repeat Row 1 once **more**.

Row 20: K7, work invisible increase, K1, work invisible increase, K8: 18 sts.

Row 21: Purl across.

Row 22: K7, work invisible increase, K3, work invisible increase, K8: 20 sts.

Row 23: Purl across.

Row 24: K7, work invisible increase, K5, work invisible increase, K8: 22 sts.

Row 25: Purl across.

Row 26: K7, slip 1, K1, PSSO, K4, K2 tog, K7: 20 sts.

Row 27: Purl across.

Row 28: K7, slip 1, K1, PSSO, K2, K2 tog, K7: 18 sts.

Row 29: Purl across.

Row 30: K7, slip 1, K1, PSSO, K2 tog, K7: 16 sts.

Row 31: P2 tog across: 8 sts.

Row 32: K2 tog across: 4 sts.

Cut yarn leaving a 15" (38 cm) length for sewing.

Thread yarn needle with end and weave through remaining sts; pull tightly and sew end of rows together. Stuff Leg, then flatten opening with seam at center back. Using photo as a guide, sew to bottom of Body.

POM-POM TAIL

Cut a piece of cardboard 3" (7.5 cm) wide and 2" (5 cm) long. Wind Pink around the cardboard lengthwise until it is approximately 1/2" (1.25 cm) thick in the middle (*Fig. A*). Carefully slip the yarn off the cardboard and firmly tie an 18" (45.5 cm) length of yarn around the middle (*Fig. B*). Leave yarn ends long enough to attach the pom-pom. Cut the loops on both ends and trim the pom-pom into a 1 1/2" (4 cm) smooth ball (*Fig. C*).

Sew Pom-pom Tail to back of Body.

Fig. A

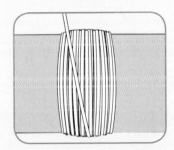

Fig. B

Fig. C

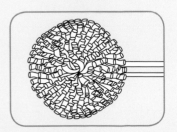

He's a bear with his own kind of focus. He'll go wherever his friends go and do all the stuff they want to do— as long as it's his idea. If you can gently lead him into an idea, you may convince him that he thought of it first. After that, everything's fine and Boyce will have a better time than anyone else. Here's an interesting bit of trivia—Boyce makes the very best honey-baked Boston beans. If the Bean Trio agrees to do a cookout and you're invited, be sure to be there!

boyce BRUIN

Finished Size: 10½" (26.5 cm) tall

MATERIALS

Medium Weight Yarn
[5 ounces, 260 yards
(141 grams, 238 meters) per skein]:
Lt Brown - 1 skein
[6 ounces, 312 yards
(170 grams, 285 meters) per skein]:
Lt Blue - 1 skein
Brown - 1 skein
Straight knitting needles, size 4 (3.5 mm)
Yarn needle
Polyester stuffing
Felt - small amount of Lt Blue and Brown
9 mm Black doll eyes - 2
Embroidery needle
Sewing needle and Brown thread

Techniques used:
- Invisible increase (*Fig. 1, page 110*)
- K2 tog (*Fig. 3, page 110*)
- P2 tog (*Fig. 5, page 110*)
- Slip 1 as if to **knit**, K1, PSSO (*Fig. 4, page 110*)

BODY AND HEAD

With Lt Brown and beginning at bottom of Body, cast on 6 sts.

Row 1 (Wrong side): Purl across.

Row 2 (Increase row): (Work invisible increase, K1) across: 12 sts.

Row 3: Purl across.

Rows 4-7: Repeat Rows 2 and 3 twice: 48 sts.

Row 8: Knit across.

Row 9: Purl across.

Rows 10-21: Repeat Rows 8 and 9, 6 times.

Cut Lt Brown.

Row 22: With Brown, knit across.

Row 23: Purl across; cut Brown.

Row 24: With Lt Blue, knit across.

Row 25: Purl across.

Rows 26-33: Repeat Rows 24 and 25, 4 times; at end of Row 33, cut Lt Blue.

Row 34: With Brown, knit across.

Instructions continued on page 90.

Row 35: Purl across; cut Brown.

Row 36: With Lt Brown, knit across.

Row 37: Purl across.

Rows 38-53: Repeat Rows 36 and 37, 8 times.

Row 54 (Decrease row): K2 tog across: 24 sts.

Row 55: Purl across.

Rows 56-58: Repeat Rows 54 and 55 once, then repeat Row 54 once **more**: 6 sts.

Cut Lt Brown leaving a 15" (38 cm) length for sewing.

Thread yarn needle with end and weave through remaining sts; pull tightly and sew end of rows together to Brown.

Trace flower pattern below and cut 2 flowers from Lt Blue felt.

Flower pattern

Insert shank of doll eye through center of felt flower. Using photo as a guide, page 91, attach eyes to face.
Finish sewing seam, stuffing firmly as you go.

With Brown and referring to photo as a guide for placement, add satin stitch nose (*Fig. 7, page 111*).

Trace ear pattern below and cut 2 ears from Brown felt. Fold ear in half and sew around outer edge, stuffing lightly. Using photo as a guide for placement, sew ears to Head.

Ear pattern

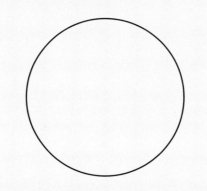

ARM (Make 2)

With Lt Brown, leaving a long end for sewing and beginning at hand, cast on 4 sts.

Row 1 (Wrong side): Purl across.

Row 2 (Increase row): (Work invisible increase, K1) across: 8 sts.

Row 3: Purl across.

Rows 4 and 5: Repeat Rows 2 and 3: 16 sts.

Row 6: Knit across.

Row 7: Purl across.

Rows 8-11: Repeat Rows 6 and 7 twice; at end of Row 11, cut Lt Brown.

Row 12: With Brown, knit across.

Row 13: Purl across; cut Brown.

Row 14: With Lt Blue, knit across.

Row 15: Purl across.

Rows 16-23: Repeat Rows 14 and 15, 4 times; at end of Row 23, cut Lt Blue.

Row 24: With Brown, knit across.

Bind off all sts in **purl**.

Thread yarn needle with long end and sew end of rows together using corresponding colors. Stuff Arm, then flatten opening with seam at center of bottom. Using photo as a guide, sew to Body along top Brown stripe.

LEG (Make 2)
With Lt Brown and beginning at top of Leg, cast on 16 sts.

Row 1: Purl across.

Row 2 (Right side): Knit across.

Rows 3-19: Repeat Rows 1 and 2, 8 times; then repeat Row 1 once **more**.

Row 20: K7, work invisible increase, K1, work invisible increase, K8: 18 sts.

Row 21: Purl across.

Row 22: K7, work invisible increase, K3, work invisible increase, K8: 20 sts.

Row 23: Purl across.

Row 24: K7, work invisible increase, K5, work invisible increase, K8: 22 sts.

Row 25: Purl across.

Row 26: K7, slip 1, K1, PSSO, K4, K2 tog, K7: 20 sts.

Row 27: Purl across.

Row 28: K7, slip 1, K1, PSSO, K2, K2 tog, K7: 18 sts.

Row 29: Purl across.

Row 30: K7, slip 1, K1, PSSO, K2 tog, K7: 16 sts.

Row 31: P2 tog across: 8 sts.

Row 32: K2 tog across: 4 sts.

Cut yarn leaving a 15" (38 cm) length for sewing.

Thread yarn needle with end and weave through remaining sts; pull tightly and sew end of rows together. Stuff Leg, then flatten opening with seam at center back. Using photo as a guide, sew to bottom of Body.

Hear that knocking sound? That's Thaddeus' knees. He can't believe his friends are considering two of the most deadly destinations in the world. Yellowstone National Park! The Canadian wilderness! Haven't they heard about the wild wolves running around out there? You see, a popular bedtime story Thaddeus read as a child has had a long-term effect on him. (You have to wonder about parents who would let a piglet read such a story.) But Thaddeus will be okay. He's already switched out everyone's airline tickets. They're going to The Big Apple—they just don't know it yet. That's why Thaddeus's knees are still knocking. He hates to hear Boyce growl and grumble. Sometimes that bear can sound just like a wolf.

thaddeus
TROTTER

Finished Size: 10¹/₂" (26.5 cm) tall

MATERIALS
Medium Weight Yarn
[6 ounces, 312 yards
(170 grams, 285 meters) per skein]:
　　Pink - 1 skein
　　Dk Pink - 1 skein
[5 ounces, 260 yards
(141 grams, 238 meters) per skein]:
　　Brown - 1 skein
Straight knitting needles, size 4 (3.5 mm)
Yarn needle
Polyester stuffing
9 mm Black doll eyes - 2
Felt - small amount of Pink
Pink embroidery floss
Embroidery needle
Sewing needle and Pink thread

Techniques used:
- Invisible increase (*Fig. 1, page 110*)
- K2 tog (*Fig. 3, page 110*)
- P2 tog (*Fig. 5, page 110*)
- Slip 1 as if to **knit**, K1, PSSO (*Fig. 4, page 110*)

BODY AND HEAD
With Pink and beginning at bottom of Body, cast on 6 sts.

Row 1 (Wrong side)**:** Purl across.

Row 2 (Increase row)**:** (Work invisible increase, K1) across: 12 sts.

Row 3: Purl across.

Rows 4-7: Repeat Rows 2 and 3 twice: 48 sts.

Row 8: Knit across.

Row 9: Purl across.

Rows 10-21: Repeat Rows 8 and 9, 6 times.

Cut Pink.

Rows 22 and 23: With Brown, knit across; at end of Row 23, drop Brown.

Row 24: With Dk Pink, knit across.

Row 25: Purl across; drop Dk Pink.

Row 26: With Brown, knit across.

Row 27: Purl across; drop Brown.

Rows 28-33: Repeat Rows 24-27 once, then repeat Rows 24 and 25 once **more**; at end of Row 33, cut Dk Pink.

Instructions continued on page 94.

Rows 34 and 35: With Brown, knit across; at end of Row 35, cut Brown.

Row 36: With Pink, knit across.

Row 37: Purl across.

Rows 38-53: Repeat Rows 36 and 37, 8 times.

Row 54 (Decrease row): K2 tog across: 24 sts.

Row 55: Purl across.

Rows 56-58: Repeat Rows 54 and 55 once, then repeat Row 54 once **more**: 6 sts.

Cut Pink leaving a 15" (38 cm) length for sewing.

Thread yarn needle with end and weave through remaining sts; pull tightly and sew end of rows together to Brown.

Using photo as a guide, page 92, attach eyes to face. Using corresponding colors, finish sewing seam, stuffing firmly as you go.

Trace nose pattern below and cut one nose from Pink felt. Using photo as a guide for placement, sew nose to face. Using straight stitch *(Fig. 8, page 111)* and embroidery needle and floss, add nostrils to nose.

Nose pattern

EAR (Make 2)
With Dk Pink, cast on 16 sts.

Row 1 (Wrong side): Purl across.

Row 2: (Slip 1, K1, PSSO, K4, K2 tog) twice: 12 sts.

Row 3: Purl across.

Row 4: (Slip 1, K1, PSSO, K2, K2 tog) twice: 8 sts.

Row 5: Purl across.

Row 6: (Slip 1, K1, PSSO, K2 tog) twice: 4 sts.

Cut Dk Pink leaving a 15" (38 cm) length for sewing.

Thread yarn needle with end and weave through remaining sts; pull tightly and sew end of rows together; do not stuff. Flatten Ear with seam at edge. Using photo as a guide, sew Ears to Head.

ARM (Make 2)
With Pink, leaving a long end for sewing and beginning at hand, cast on 4 sts.

Row 1 (Wrong side): Purl across.

Row 2 (Increase row): (Work invisible increase, K1) across: 8 sts.

Row 3: Purl across.

Rows 4 and 5: Repeat Rows 2 and 3: 16 sts.

Row 6: Knit across.

Row 7: Purl across.

Rows 8 and 9: Repeat Rows 6 and 7; at end of Row 9, cut Pink.

Rows 10 and 11: With Brown, knit across; at end of Row 11, drop Brown.

Row 12: With Dk Pink, knit across.

Row 13: Purl across; drop Dk Pink.

Row 14: With Brown, knit across.

Row 15: Purl across; drop Brown.

Rows 16-21: Repeat Rows 12-15 once, then repeat Rows 12 and 13 once **more**; at end of Row 21, cut Dk Pink.

Row 22: With Brown, knit across.

Bind off all sts in **purl**.

Thread yarn needle with long end and sew end of rows together using corresponding colors. Stuff Arm, then flatten opening with seam at center of bottom. Using photo as a guide, sew to Body along top Brown stripe.

LEG (Make 2)
With Pink and beginning at top of Leg, cast on 16 sts.

Row 1: Purl across.

Row 2 (Right side): Knit across.

Rows 3-19: Repeat Rows 1 and 2, 8 times; then repeat Row 1 once **more**.

Row 20: K2 tog across: 8 sts.

Row 21: Purl across.

Row 22: K2 tog across: 4 sts.

Cut yarn leaving a 15" (38 cm) length for sewing.

Thread yarn needle with end and weave through remaining sts; pull tightly and sew end of rows together. Stuff Leg, then flatten opening with seam at ceter back. Using photo as a guide, sew to bottom of Body.

TAIL
With Dk Pink, cast on 24 sts.

Row 1: Knit across.

Row 2: K2 tog across: 12 sts.

Row 3: K2 tog across: 6 sts.

Bind off remaining sts.

Sew Tail to back of Body.

fishbowl FRIENDS

S o-o-o, Dude, the clerk at the pet store didn't tell you that clownfish can't tolerate fresh water? Bummer. He should have pointed you toward the larger aquariums with the glass-topped canopies. They can be set up with the right kind of water. Oh, and it looks like the clownfish taught the angelfish how to jump out of the bowl. The goldfish is checking this out, too. Hmmm. Maybe you could get a couple more fishbowls and put them side-by-side. That way, the girls could just "hop" from one bowl to the other. Yeah! After a while, you could place the bowls farther apart. Afraid they might not make the jump? Worry not. Let the girls watch some B-ball on your TV. Then, just put a hoop above each fishbowl. Bet they'll make 2-pointers every time. Cool!

O ne moment she's the Queen of the Amazon River. The next, she's in a puny fishbowl. "It ain't right," she says. Amy's got a lot of vim and vigor, and one dumpy little bowl doesn't do it for her. Sure, the flaked fish food is pretty tasty, and she doesn't have to fight her 300 sisters for every morsel. Angelfish are an outgoing group like that. But here, her neighbors are just too passive. The goldfish acts like her little fishbowl is a mansion, which is irritating. On the other fin, the clownfish has some kind of issue with the lack of salt in the water. "Specific gravity and lack of supportive substrate," or some such nonsense. Yadda, yadda, yadda. However, Amy jumped the moment she saw the clownfish bail out. She wasn't about to stick around if bigger, better water could be found.

amy
ANGELFISH

Finished Size: 8¹/₂" (21.5 cm) tall

MATERIALS
Medium Weight Yarn
[3¹/₂ ounces, 170 yards
(100 grams, 156 meters) per skein]:
  Yellow - 1 skein
  Blue - 1 skein
  Black - small amount for mouth
Straight knitting needles, size 4 (3.5 mm)
Yarn needle
Polyester stuffing
9 mm Black doll eyes - 2

Techniques used:
• Invisible increase *(Fig. 1, page 110)*
• K2 tog *(Fig. 3, page 110)*
• P2 tog *(Fig. 5, page 110)*

BODY
With Yellow and beginning at mouth, cast on 4 sts.

Row 1 (Wrong side): Purl across.

Row 2 (Increase row): (Work invisible increase, K1) across: 8 sts.

Row 3: Purl across.

Row 4: ★ Work invisible increase, K3, work invisible increase, K1; repeat from ★ once **more**: 12 sts.

Row 5: Purl across.

Row 6: ★ Work invisible increase, K5, work invisible increase, K1; repeat from ★ once **more**: 16 sts.

Row 7: Purl across.

Row 8: ★ Work invisible increase, K7, work invisible increase, K1; repeat from ★ once **more**: 20 sts.

Row 9: Purl across; drop Yellow.

Row 10: With Blue, ★ work invisible increase, K9, work invisible increase, K1; repeat from ★ once **more**: 24 sts.

Row 11: Purl across; cut Blue.

Row 12: With Yellow, ★ work invisible increase, K 11, work invisible increase, K1; repeat from ★ once **more**: 28 sts.

Row 13: Purl across.

Instructions continued on page 100.

Row 14: ★ Work invisible increase, K 13, work invisible increase, K1; repeat from ★ once **more**: 32 sts.

Row 15: Purl across.

Row 16: ★ Work invisible increase, K 15, work invisible increase, K1; repeat from ★ once **more**: 36 sts.

Row 17: Purl across; cut Yellow.

Row 18: With Blue, ★ work invisible increase, K 17, work invisible increase, K1; repeat from ★ once **more**: 40 sts.

Row 19: Purl across.

Row 20: ★ Work invisible increase, K 19, work invisible increase, K1; repeat from ★ once **more**; cut Blue: 44 sts.

Row 21: With Yellow, purl across.

Row 22: ★ Work invisible increase, K 21, work invisible increase, K1; repeat from ★ once **more**: 48 sts.

Row 23: Purl across.

Row 24: ★ Work invisible increase, K 23, work invisible increase, K1; repeat from ★ once **more**: 52 sts.

Row 25: Purl across.

Row 26: ★ Work invisible increase, K 25, work invisible increase, K1; repeat from ★ once **more**; drop Yellow: 56 sts.

Row 27: With Blue, purl across.

Row 28: ★ Work invisible increase, K 27, work invisible increase, K1; repeat from ★ once **more**: 60 sts.

Row 29: Purl across.

Row 30: ★ Work invisible increase, K 29, work invisible increase, K1; repeat from ★ once **more**; cut Blue: 64 sts.

Row 31: With Yellow, purl across.

Row 32: ★ Work invisible increase, K 31, work invisible increase, K1; repeat from ★ once **more**: 68 sts.

Row 33: Purl across.

Row 34: ★ Work invisible increase, K 33, work invisible increase, K1; repeat from ★ once **more**: 72 sts.

Row 35: Purl across.

Row 36: ★ Work invisible increase, K 35, work invisible increase, K1; repeat from ★ once **more**; cut Yellow: 76 sts.

Row 37: With Blue, purl across.

Row 38: ★ Work invisible increase, K 37, work invisible increase, K1; repeat from ★ once **more**: 80 sts.

Row 39: Purl across.

Row 40: Work invisible increase, (K1, work invisible increase) twice, K 35, work invisible increase, (K1, work invisible increase) 5 times, K 35, (work invisible increase, K1) 3 times: 92 sts.

Bind off all sts in **purl**.

Using photo as a guide for placement, page 98, attach eyes.

With corresponding color yarn, sew bottom and back seam, stuffing firmly as you go.

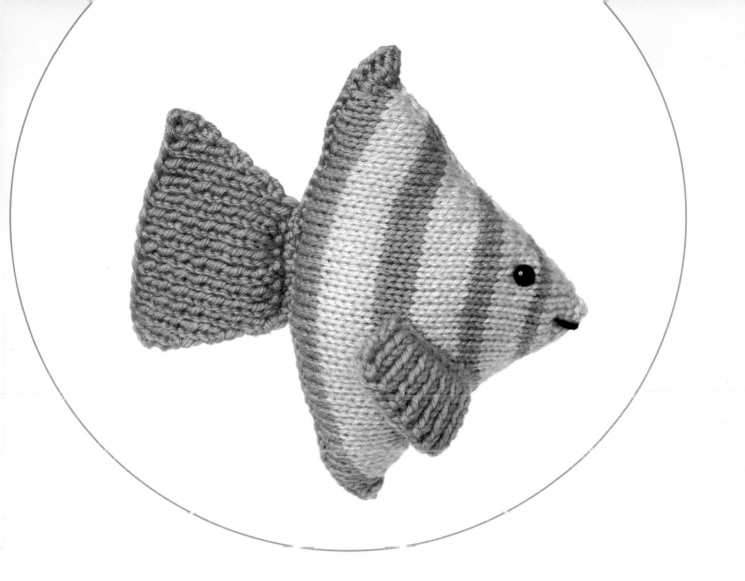

BACK TAIL FIN
With Blue, cast on 30 sts.

Row 1 (Wrong side)**:** (P1, K1) across.

Row 2 (Decrease row)**:** K2 tog, (P1, K1) across to last 2 sts, P2 tog: 28 sts.

Row 3: (K1, P1) across.

Row 4 (Decrease row)**:** P2 tog, (K1, P1) across to last 2 sts, K2 tog: 26 sts.

Row 5: (P1, K1) across.

Rows 6-15: Repeat Rows 2-5 twice, then repeat Rows 2 and 3 once **more**: 16 sts.

Row 16: K2 tog across: 8 sts.

Bind off remaining sts in **purl**.

Using photo as a guide, sew bound off edge to back of Body.

SIDE FIN (Make 2)
With Blue, cast on 16 sts.

Rows 1-8: (P1, K1) across.

Row 9: K2 tog across: 8 sts.

Bind off remaining sts in **purl**.

Using photo as a guide for placement, sew bound off edge to side of Body.

With Black, sew mouth using straight stitch *(Fig. 8, page 111)*.

Cora is a patient fish, but goodness! That Amy Angelfish will take some getting used to. Now, Gloria Goldfish is just fine. Cora likes her quiet nature. It's the water in Gloria's bowl that just won't work. It's all wrong. Cora had to get out of there. If she could dial the phone, she'd call the ASPCA. Wait a minute. Is that the new owner? Coming with another fishbowl? No, he has two more fishbowls! They each get their own bowl! And yes, one has salt water. Well, it's a start. Cora can settle in now. Maybe there will be a big tank with an anemone in her near future. Wait a minute. What's with the big ring positioned above her new bowl of salt water? That's a puzzler.

cora
CLOWNFISH

Finished Size: 4" (10 cm) tall

MATERIALS

Medium Weight Yarn
[3½ ounces, 170 yards
(100 grams, 156 meters) per skein]:
  Orange - 1 skein
  White - 1 skein
  Black - 1 skein
Straight knitting needles, size 4 (3.5 mm)
Yarn needle
Polyester stuffing
9 mm Black doll eyes - 2

Techniques used:

• Invisible increase *(Fig. 1, page 110)*
• K2 tog *(Fig. 3, page 110)*

BODY

With Black and beginning at tail end of Body, cast on 6 sts.

Row 1 (Wrong side)**:** Purl across; drop Black.

Row 2 (Increase row)**:** With White, (work invisible increase, K1) across: 12 sts.

Row 3: Purl across.

Row 4: (Work invisible increase, K2) across: 18 sts.

Row 5: Purl across; cut White.

Row 6: With Black, (work invisible increase, K3) across: 24 sts.

Row 7: Purl across; cut Black.

Row 8: With Orange, (work invisible increase, K4) across: 30 sts.

Row 9: Purl across.

Row 10: (Work invisible increase, K5) across: 36 sts.

Row 11: Purl across.

Row 12: Knit across.

Rows 13-15: Repeat Rows 11 and 12 once, then repeat Row 11 once **more**; at end of Row 15; cut Orange.

Row 16: With Black, knit across.

Row 17: Purl across; drop Black.

Instructions continued on page 104.

Row 18: With White, knit across.

Row 19: Purl across.

Rows 20 and 21: Repeat Rows 18 and 19; at end of Row 21, cut White.

Row 22: With Black, knit across.

Row 23: Purl across; cut Black.

Row 24: With Orange, knit across.

Row 25: Purl across.

Rows 26-31: Repeat Rows 24 and 25, 3 times; at end of Row 31, cut Orange.

Row 32: With Black, knit across.

Row 33: Purl across; drop Black.

Row 34: With White, (K2 tog, K7) across: 32 sts.

Row 35: Purl across.

Row 36: (K2 tog, K6) across: 28 sts.

Row 37: Purl across; cut White.

Row 38: With Black, (K2 tog, K5) across: 24 sts.

Row 39: Purl across; cut Black.

Row 40: With Orange, (K2 tog, K4) across: 20 sts.

Row 41: Purl across.

Row 42: (K2 tog, K3) across: 16 sts.

Row 43: Purl across.

Row 44: (K2 tog, K2) across: 12 sts.

Row 45: Purl across.

Row 46: (K2 tog, K1) across: 8 sts.

Row 47: Purl across.

Row 48: K2 tog across: 4 sts.

Cut yarn leaving a 15" (38 cm) length for sewing.

Thread yarn needle with end and weave through remaining sts; pull tightly. Using corresponding colors, sew end of rows together halfway.

Using photo as a guide for placement, page 105, attach eyes. Finish sewing seam, stuffing firmly as you go.

BACK TAIL FIN
With White, cast on 16 sts.

Row 1 (Wrong side)**:** (P1, K1) across; cut White.

Rows 2 and 3: With Black, (P1, K1) across; at end of Row 3, cut Black.

Rows 4-8: With Orange, (P1, K1) across.

Row 9: K2 tog across: 8 sts.

Bind off remaining sts in **purl**.

Using photo as a guide, sew bound off edge to back of Body.

SIDE FIN (Make 2)
With Orange, cast on 2 sts.

Row 1: Knit across.

Row 2: Slip 1 as if to **purl**, work invisible increase, K1: 3 sts.

Row 3: Knit across.

Row 4: Slip 1 as if to **purl**, K1, work invisible increase, K1: 4 sts.

Row 5: Knit across.

Row 6 (Increase row)**:** Slip 1 as if to **purl**, knit across to last st, work invisible increase, K1: 5 sts.

Row 7: Knit across.

Rows 8 and 9: Repeat Rows 6 and 7: 6 sts.

Row 10: Slip 1 as if to **purl**, knit across.

Row 11: Knit across.

Rows 12 and 13: Repeat Rows 10 and 11.

Bind off remaining sts in **knit**.

Using photo as a guide for placement, sew one Side Fin to each side of Body.

SMALL FRONT FIN (Make 3)
With Orange, cast on 10 sts.

Row 1: K2 tog, (P1, K1) across: 9 sts.

Row 2: P1, (K1, P1) 3 times, K2 tog: 8 sts.

Row 3: K2 tog, (P1, K1) across: 7 sts.

Bind off remaining sts in pattern.

Using photo as a guide: Sew cast on edge of one Small Front Fin to top of Body, having the decrease edge toward the head.

Sew remaining two Small Front Fins to bottom of Body with decrease edge at center bottom and opposite edge angled toward side.

LARGE BACK FIN (Make 2)
With Orange, cast on 10 sts.

Row 1: K2 tog, (P1, K1) across: 9 sts.

Row 2: P1, (K1, P1) 3 times, K2 tog: 8 sts.

Row 3: K2 tog, (P1, K1) across: 7 sts.

Row 4: P1, (K1, P1) twice, K2 tog: 6 sts.

Row 5: K2 tog, (P1, K1) twice: 5 sts.

Bind off remaining sts in pattern.

Using photo as a guide: Sew cast on edge of one Large Back Fin to top of Body, having the decrease edge toward the head.

Sew remaining Large Back Fin to bottom of Body in the same manner.

So, Owner thinks Gloria will jump through hoops? Not likely. It's thoughtful of him to offer, but Gloria is happy to sit in her bowl and admire the pretty glass pebbles. The new girls, though—they're the kinds who want to go places and do things. As long as Gloria's bowl is in the same room with a television, she's set for life. Oh, look! Owner is switching on the TV! What's on? Ah, March Madness! Owner is such a basketball fan. It's fun to see him throw corn chips everywhere when his team scores. Maybe some will land in Gloria's bowl.

gloria
GOLDFISH

Finished Size: 5" (12.5 cm) tall

MATERIALS
Medium Weight Yarn
[3½ ounces, 170 yards
(100 grams, 156 meters) per skein]:
   Orange - 1 skein
Straight knitting needles, size 4 (3.5 mm)
Yarn needle
Polyester stuffing
9 mm Black doll eyes - 2

Techniques used:
• Invisible increase *(Fig. 1, page 110)*
• K2 tog *(Fig. 3, page 110)*
• Slip 1 as if to **knit**, K1, PSSO *(Fig. 4, page 110)*

BODY
With Orange and beginning at tail end of Body, cast on 6 sts.

Row 1 (Wrong side): Purl across.

Row 2 (Increase row): (Work invisible increase, K1) across: 12 sts.

Row 3: Purl across.

Rows 4 and 5: Repeat Rows 2 and 3: 24 sts.

Row 6: (Work invisible increase, K2) across: 36 sts.

Row 7: Purl across.

Row 8: (Work invisible increase, K3) across: 48 sts.

Row 9: Purl across.

Row 10: Knit across.

Row 11: Purl across.

Rows 12-27: Repeat Rows 10 and 11, 8 times.

Row 28: (K2 tog, K4) across. 40 sts.

Row 29: Purl across.

Row 30: (K2 tog, K3) across: 32 sts.

Row 31: Purl across.

Row 32: (K2 tog, K2) across: 24 sts.

Row 33: Purl across.

Row 34: (K2 tog, K1) across: 16 sts.

Row 35: Purl across.

Row 36: K2 tog across: 8 sts.

Row 37: Purl across.

Row 38: K2 tog across: 4 sts.

Cut yarn leaving a 15" (38 cm) length for sewing.

Thread yarn needle with end and weave through remaining sts; pull tightly and sew end of rows together halfway.

Using photo as a guide for placement, page 108, attach eyes. Finish sewing seam, stuffing firmly as you go.

BACK TAIL FIN (Make 2)
With Orange, cast on 20 sts.

Row 1 (Wrong side): Purl across.

Row 2 (Decrease row): Slip 1, K1, PSSO, knit across to last 2 sts, K2 tog: 18 sts.

Instructions continued on page 108.

Rows 3-10: Repeat Rows 1 and 2, 4 times: 10 sts.

Bind off remaining sts in **purl**.

With **wrong** sides together and matching cast on and bound off edges, sew seam around entire fin stuffing lightly before closing.

Using photo as a guide, sew bound off edge to back of Body.

TOP FIN
With Orange, cast on 24 sts.

Row 1 (Wrong side): Purl across.

Row 2 (Decrease row): (Slip 1, K1, PSSO) twice, knit across to last 4 sts, K2 tog twice: 20 sts.

Row 3: Purl across.

Rows 4-9: Repeat Rows 2 and 3, 3 times: 8 sts.

Row 10: K2 tog across: 4 sts.

Cut yarn leaving a 15" (38 cm) length for sewing.

Thread yarn needle with end and weave through remaining sts; pull tightly and sew end of rows together; stuff Top Fin lightly then sew cast on edge together. Sew cast on edge to top of Body.

SIDE FIN (Make 2)
With Orange, cast on 16 sts.

Row 1 (Wrong side): Purl across.

Row 2: Knit across.

Rows 3-5: Repeat Rows 1 and 2 once, then repeat Row 1 once **more**.

Row 6: K2 tog across: 8 sts.

Row 7: Purl across.

Row 8: K2 tog across: 4 sts.

Cut yarn leaving a 15" (38 cm) length for sewing.

Thread yarn needle with end and weave through remaining sts; pull tightly and sew end of rows together; stuff Side Fin lightly then sew cast on edge together. Sew cast on edge to side of Body.

general
INSTRUCTIONS

KNITTING NEEDLES		
UNITED STATES	ENGLISH U.K.	METRIC (mm)
0	13	2
1	12	2.25
2	11	2.75
3	10	3.25
4	9	3.5
5	8	3.75
6	7	4
7	6	4.5
8	5	5
9	4	5.5
10	3	6
10½	2	6.5
11	1	8
13	00	9
15	000	10
17	---	12.75

KNIT TERMINOLOGY	
UNITED STATES	INTERNATIONAL
gauge =	tension
bind off =	cast off
yarn over (YO) =	yarn forward (yfwd) or yarn around needle (yrn)

ABBREVIATIONS

cm	centimeters
K	knit
mm	millimeters
P	purl
PSSO	pass slipped stitch over
st(s)	stitch(es)
tog	together
WYB	with yarn in back
WYF	with yarn in front

★ — work instructions following ★ as many **more** times as indicated in addition to the first time.

( ) or [ ] — work enclosed instructions **as many** times as specified by the number immediately following **or** contains explanatory remarks.

colon (:) — the number given after a colon at the end of a row denotes the number of stitches you should have on that row.

Yarn Weight Symbol & Names	LACE 0	SUPER FINE 1	FINE 2	LIGHT 3	MEDIUM 4	BULKY 5	SUPER BULKY 6
Type of Yarns in Category	Fingering, size 10 crochet thread	Sock, Fingering, Baby	Sport, Baby	DK, Light Worsted	Worsted, Afghan, Aran	Chunky, Craft, Rug	Bulky, Roving
Knit Gauge Range* in Stockinette St to 4" (10 cm)	33-40** sts	27-32 sts	23-26 sts	21-24 sts	16-20 sts	12-15 sts	6-11 sts
Advised Needle Size Range	000-1	1 to 3	3 to 5	5 to 7	7 to 9	9 to 11	11 and larger

*GUIDELINES ONLY: The chart above reflects the most commonly used gauges and needle sizes for specific yarn categories.

** Lace weight yarns are usually knitted on larger needles to create lacy openwork patterns. Accordingly, a gauge range is difficult to determine. Always follow the gauge stated in your pattern.

◼◻◻◻ **BEGINNER**	Projects for first-time knitters using basic knit and purl stitches. Minimal shaping.
◼◼◻◻ **EASY**	Projects using basic stitches, repetitive stitch patterns, simple color changes, and simple shaping and finishing.
◼◼◼◻ **INTERMEDIATE**	Projects with a variety of stitches, such as basic cables and lace, simple intarsia, double-pointed needles and knitting in the round needle techniques, mid-level shaping and finishing.
◼◼◼◼ **EXPERIENCED**	Projects using advanced techniques and stitches, such as short rows, fair isle, more intricate intarsia, cables, lace patterns, and numerous color changes.

GAUGE

The instructions are written for Medium Weight Yarn with some pieces made with Bulky Weight Yarn. Gauge is not of great importance; your project may be a little larger or smaller without changing the overall effect. Be sure your fabric is dense enough so that stuffing does not show through your stitches.

INCREASES
INVISIBLE INCREASE

Insert the right needle from the front into the side of the stitch on the left needle (*Fig. 1*) and knit it.

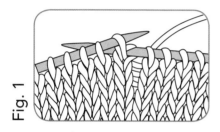

Fig. 1

KNIT INCREASE

Knit the next stitch but do **not** slip the old stitch off the left needle (*Fig. 2a*). Insert the right needle into the back loop of the same stitch and knit it (*Fig. 2b*), then slip the old stitch off the left needle.

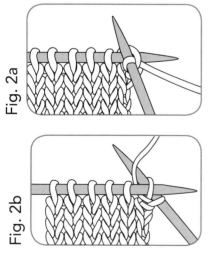

Fig. 2a

Fig. 2b

DECREASES
KNIT 2 TOGETHER
(abbreviated K2 tog)

Insert the right needle into the **front** of the first two stitches on the left needle as if to **knit** (*Fig. 3*), then knit them together.

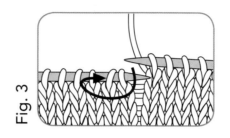

Fig. 3

SLIP 1, KNIT 1, PASS SLIPPED STITCH OVER
(abbreviated slip 1, K1, PSSO)

Slip one stitch as if to **knit**. Knit the next stitch. With the left needle, bring the slipped stitch over the knit stitch (*Fig. 4*) and off the needle.

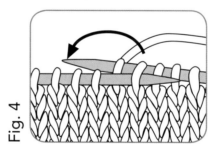

Fig. 4

PURL 2 TOGETHER
(abbreviated P2 tog)

Insert the right needle into the **front** of the first two stitches on the left needle as if to **purl** (*Fig. 5*), then purl them together.

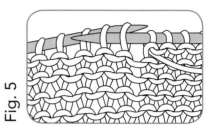

Fig. 5

KNIT 3 TOGETHER
(abbreviated K3 tog)

Insert the right needle into the **front** of the first three stitches on the left needle as if to **knit** (*Fig. 6*), then knit them together.

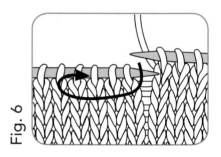

Fig. 6

EMBROIDERY STITCHES

SATIN STITCH

Satin Stitch is a series of straight stitches worked side-by-side so they touch but do not overlap. Come up at odd numbers and go down at even numbers (*Fig. 7*).

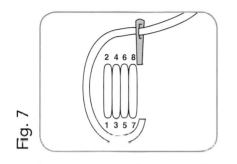

Fig. 7

STRAIGHT STITCH

Straight Stitch is just what the name implies, a single, straight stitch. Come up at 1 and go down at 2 (*Fig. 8*).

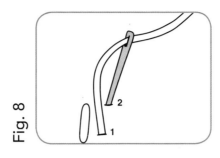

Fig. 8

FRENCH KNOT

Bring needle up at 1. Wrap yarn around the needle the desired number of times and insert needle at 2, holding end of yarn with non-stitching fingers (*Fig. 9*). Tighten knot; then pull needle through, holding yarn until it must be released.

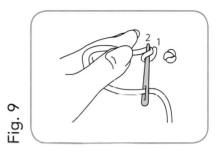

Fig. 9

YARN INFORMATION

Each item in this leaflet was made using various weights of yarn. Any brand of the specified weight of yarn may be used. It is best to refer to the yardage/meters when determining how many balls or skeins to purchase.

For your convenience, listed below are the specified yarns used to create our photography models.

FRIENDLY SEA-CIETY

CLETUS CLAW
Lion Brand® Vanna's Choice®
Dk Red - #180 Cranberry

TENTACLE TERRY
Lion Brand® Vanna's Choice®
Purple - #147 Purple

SHELLY GREEN
Lion Brand® Vanna's Choice®
Green - #174 Olive
Lt Green - #173 Dusty Green

BIG BLUE
Lion Brand® Vanna's Choice®
Dk Blue - #109 Colonial Blue
Lt Blue - #105 Silver Blue

SPRING PARTY

BIRDHOUSE & WREN TWINS
TLC® Essentials™
Lt Green - #2615 Lt Celery
Dk Brown - #2368 Dk Brown
Brown - #2335 Taupe
Lt Blue - #2820 Robin Egg
Lt Pink - #2716 Powder Pink

BUSTER BUNNY, JR.
TLC® Essentials™
Off-White - #2316 Winter White
Pink - #2716 Powder Pink

BILLIE WADDLE
Lion Brand® Vanna's Choice® Baby
Yellow - #157 Duckie
Lion Brand® Vanna's Choice®
Orange - #134 Terracotta

HAROLD (HANK) LAMBSWOOL
Lion Brand® Wool-Ease®
White - #501 White Frost
Black - #153 Black
Pink - #165 Blossom

THE BIRDS AND BEES

OLIVER WHO
Lion Brand® Vanna's Choice® Baby
Green - #169 Sweet Pea
Dk Pink - #139 Berrylicious
Coral - #132 Goldfish
Yellow - #157 Duckie
Blue - #106 Little Boy Blue
Pink - #138 Pink Poodle
White - #100 Angel White

BUZZ HOVER
Lion Brand® Vanna's Choice®
Black - #153 Black
White - #100 White
Dk Red - #180 Cranberry
Lion Brand® Vanna's Choice® Baby
Yellow - #157 Duckie

FRED LEAPER
Lion Brand® Vanna's Choice®
Green - #171 Fern
Dk Green - #172 Kelly Green
White - #100 White
Dk Red - #180 Cranberry
Lion Brand® Vanna's Choice® Baby
Lt Green - #169 Sweet Pea

LINDSAY LADYBEETLE
Lion Brand® Vanna's Choice®
Black - #153 Black
White - #100 White
Lion Brand® Vanna's Choice® Baby
Red - #114 Cheery Cherry

FOREST FRIENDS

ODESSA OWL
TLC® Essentials™
Dk Brown - #2368 Dk Brown
Brown - #2335 Taupe

HORATIO HEDGEHOG
Caron® Simply Soft®
Tan - #2604 Bone
TLC® Essentials™
Dk Brown - #2368 Dk Brown
Lion Brand® Fun Fur
Dk Brown - #126 Chocolate

CINDA SQUIRREL
TLC® Essentials™
Brown - #2335 Taupe
Dk Brown - #2368 Dk Brown
Lion Brand® Fun Fur
Rust - #134 Copper

WHITE-SPOTTED MUSHROOM
Lion Brand® Vanna's Choice®
Dk Red - #180 Cranberry
White - #100 White

PIPPA MOUSE
TLC® Heathers™
Brown - #2443 Nutmeg
TLC® Essentials™
Pink - #2772 Lt Country Rose

ERIK & GUNNAR
Lion Brand® Wool-Ease®
Green - #180 Forest Green Heather
Blue - #115 Blue Mist
Off-White - #099 Fisherman
Black - #153 Black
Red - #138 Cranberry
White - #501 White Frost

BIG-CAPPED ACORN
TLC® Essentials™
Dk Brown - #2368 Dk Brown
Caron® Simply Soft®
Tan - #2604 Bone

BEAN TRIO

HAROLD HOPPER
TLC® Essentials™
White - #2316 Winter White
Pink - #2716 Powder Pink
Lt Green - #2615 Lt Celery

BOYCE BRUIN
TLC® Heathers™
Lt Brown - #2443 Nutmeg
TLC® Essentials™
Lt Blue - #2820 Robin Egg
Brown - #2368 Dk Brown

THADDEUS TROTTER
TLC® Essentials™
Pink - #2716 Powder Pink
Dk Pink - #2772 Lt Country Rose
TLC® Essentials™
Brown - #2443 Nutmeg

FISHBOWL FRIENDS

AMY ANGELFISH
Lion Brand® Vanna's Choice® Baby
Yellow - #157 Duckie
Blue - #106 Little Boy Blue
Lion Brand® Vanna's Choice®
Black - #153 Black

CORA CLOWNFISH
Lion Brand® Vanna's Choice®
Orange - #134 Terracotta
White - #100 White
Black - #153 Black

GLORIA GOLDFISH
Lion Brand® Vanna's Choice® Baby
Orange - #132 Goldfish